MW01145994

GHOSTVILLE

Remembering
Wisconsin
Ghost Towns

J.L. Fredrick

*To Maureen—
Enjoy!
[signature]
8/19/2017*

Lovstad Publishing
www.Lovstadpublishing.com

GHOSTVILLE

Revised Edition

ISBN: 0692208372
ISBN-13: 978-0692208373

Printed in the United States of America

Cover design by Lovstad Publishing
Cover photo: c. Late 1940s/early '50s. Area known as
"Old Town" just south of Westby, Wisconsin, the original
site of that city. Building at center was a cooperage.
Township road between it and barn in background
leads to author's childhood farm home.
(These buildings no longer exist.)

Novels by J.L. Fredrick

Across the Dead Line
Across the Second Dead Line
The Private Journal of Clancy Crane
Unfinished Business
The Other End of the Tunnel
Another Shade of Gray
The Gaslight Knights
Thunder in the Night
The Great Train Robbery of Monroe County
Mad City Bust
September Ten
aftermath
Cursed by the Wind
Dance With a Tornado

Non-Fiction
Rivers, Roads, & Rails

CONTENTS

GHOSTVILLE

Remembering Wisconsin Ghost Towns

In a not-so-distant past, Wisconsin was dotted with countless embryo settlements, many of them existing as the result of a single log cabin in the wilderness that served as a dwelling for its occupants, and may have doubled as a general store or trading post. In most all cases, that single log cabin, so far removed from any other civilization, there would be a standing welcome to any and all weary travelers needing protection from the elements for a night, making that cabin's role a motel. Of course, the accommodations were not to include all the creature comforts that we, today, enjoy when visiting locales away from our familiar surroundings of home, but neither did it include any cost to the traveler. If the traveler was lucky, he might find himself grateful for enough vacant space on a floor, upon which he could roll up in his own blanket, if he had one with him, or at least warm himself near a fire on a cold night. If food was available—dependent on the cabin owner's hunting, gathering, and/or gardening skills—it would undoubtedly be shared with the traveler guest.

Our traveler was, perhaps, in route to his own envisioned utopia, that place where he anticipated the erection of another cabin that would become his home. He would till the adjacent lands and grow crops; he would hunt game in the surrounding forests and net fish from a nearby stream. One day he, too, would welcome in a stranger seeking shelter from the chilly darkness, and share with him the spoils of the last hunting expedition.

From these meager beginnings sprouted settlements where the conditions provided ample resources. Land rights were acquired by the early settler who laid the plans for his town. As more people arrived and populated the settlement, various talents and professions came with them, and the town would soon boast blacksmith shops, sawmills, gristmills, wagon and harness makers, mercantile stores, hotels, butcher shops, boot and shoe shops— businesses essential to the survival of the community. In time, when and if the population continued to increase, the commercial arena likewise gained momentum with more varied and specialized enterprise. With growth also came the social and intellectual installations of schools, churches, libraries and places of entertainment such as opera houses. And don't forget the houses of indulgence—the brothels and saloons and gambling houses that were commonplace fixtures in many frontier towns.

By the early 1800s a number of hardy pioneers had penetrated this new country, settling mostly along rivers and streams, and in the southwestern lead mining region. Many were little more than hunters and trappers, while some actually cleared and cultivated the land. Most of these settlers had no more than footpaths leading to their solitary cabins in the unbroken forest.

The Wisconsin Territory was designated in 1836; Statehood came in 1848. By then, emigration into the region was in full swing, and the early pioneers soon found themselves with neighbors. Farmers from the crowded Eastern seaboard seeking cheap land cleared away the forest; businessmen of all sorts located and developed towns, built dams and erected mills, sawed logs into lumber for homes, laid out roads and established ferry service across the waterways. The solitude of the wilderness was interrupted, but these high-spirited early settlers bridged the way into Wisconsin's incredible future.

All settlements, of course, did not mature to large, important cities. Some didn't survive for various reasons. But they all surely experienced grand moments, when anticipation of greatness loomed and prosperity seemed well within grasp.

Come with me now on this virtual tour of days gone by at some of Wisconsin's little-known but memorable places, and experience...

GHOSTVILLE

BEFORE IT WAS WISCONSIN

GLACIERS
and
WISCONSIN'S LANDSCAPE

W hat is now Wisconsin laid beneath the immense weight of a vast sea about 500 million years ago. During that time, Wisconsin history began as the tremendous pressure of the seawater turned the sand to rock— sandstone, to be more precise.

Then, 499 million years later, the ice age began, bringing four monolithic glaciers descending from the northern polar cap, flattening entire mountain ranges, pulverizing them to boulders, pebbles and sand. They carved and scoured the surface, and in some places gouged huge pockets into the earth as they progressed southward. This bulldozing action transformed Wisconsin's mountainous landscape into rolling hills and flatland in comparison to the original terrain, pushing miles and miles of dirt, rock and debris into mounds called a moraine.

Most of Wisconsin lay beneath these massive glaciers. And then, after thousands of years, the temperatures rose and the glaciers receded, ending the ice age. In their wake they deposited boulders, rubble and other debris that had been trapped deep within the miles-thick ice, and the melt water filled the carved pockets and craters forming thousands of lakes and countless acres of marshland that have become integral parts of Wisconsin history.

A very profound aspect of Wisconsin history and its varied landscape occurred in the area that didn't experience glacial coverage. It is called the "driftless area" and includes the western and southwestern portion of the state. This area was merely surrounded by glaciers; it was spared from glacial grinding and pulverization. But the melt water floods created fast-moving rivers that carved their own passages and sculpted some of the most remarkable rock formations in America. Much of the driftless area is rough, rocky terrain, characterized by craggy, elevated cliffs.

It stands to reason, then, that much of the present-day Wisconsin landscape was created by the effects of ice. But that's not all the ice did; it carried with it seeds among all that rubble and debris, deposited them in the soil with the melting, and as temperatures rose, the seeds sprouted and grew, creating a vast area of dense forest and grasslands.

If the ice age was one of the most catastrophic events in the history of this planet, it left behind one of the most incredible landscapes of the modern world.

THE POPULATION EVOLVES

Over 12,000 years ago, just after the glacial ice receded, the first people to live in the area that is now Wisconsin were the Paleo Indians. Hunters and gatherers, they were the first of five culture stages that inhabited the region prior to the arrival of the first European explorers. As the environment changed with the aging of the earth, so did the culture. The next stage—those who lived in the region during the most drastic change—were known as the Archaic Indians, nomadic hunters who fashioned tools from rock.

A more advanced people followed: the Early Woodland culture moved in about 800 B.C. They stored their food supplies, made clay pottery, and buried their dead in mounds. This more sophisticated practice of mound building continued with the Middle and Late Woodland periods, as well. The Late Woodland people created burial mounds in the shapes of animals and birds called effigy mounds that have been discovered throughout southern Wisconsin.

Another cultural group entered Wisconsin during the last few hundred years of the effigy mound era. The Middle Mississippians migrated to

Wisconsin from a powerful nation to the south. Their primary city of Cahokia, located across the river from present-day St. Louis, Missouri had a population of some 35,000 people, one of the largest cities in the world at that time. Their uniqueness set them apart from other tribes as they had established trade routes that extended from the Gulf of Mexico to the Great Lakes, and the Atlantic coast to the Rocky Mountains. They settled in two locations in Wisconsin: Aztalan, about mid-way between present-day Madison and Milwaukee along the little Crawfish River; and a city near present-day Trempealeau on the Upper Mississippi River. Both cities were mysteriously abandoned by about 1200 A.D. (You will find more about Aztalan in a later chapter.)

And yet another culture similar to the Mississippians appeared at this time in southern Wisconsin. The Oneota differed from the Mississippians in that they rarely built burial mounds, and they left behind etched pictographic writing on rock walls, indicating that they had advanced to at least a limited written language.

When the first European explorers arrived in Wisconsin, the inhabitants they discovered were the descendants of the Oneota and the Late

Woodlanders. The Chippewa were in the north around Lake Superior, the Potawatomi occupied western Wisconsin, and the Menominee, Winnebago, Sauk, Fox and Miami were scattered throughout the entire territory.

All these different tribes practiced farming to some degree, planting crops of corn, squash and beans. Those living in the far north had much shorter growing seasons, so naturally they were more dependent on hunting and fishing for their main source of food. And they all harvested wild rice, nuts, berries, and fruit indigenous to their areas.

As more Europeans immigrated to America, and more of the land on the eastern seaboard was developed and settled, the Native American tribes were pushed farther west. Eventually, Wisconsin inherited some of that population. Among these "refugee" tribes were the Sauk, Mascoutin, Potawatomi, Kickapoo, Ojibwa, Ottawa, and Fox. The influx of these "new" tribes moving into the region did not come without conflict; there were many clashes over territory, and with the introduction of the European fur trade, competition for hunting and trapping grounds caused even more conflict.

EARLY EXPLORERS

Jean Nicolet, a young, adventurous Frenchman came to New France (Canada) in 1618 when Quebec and Montreal were just infant settlements. The governor of New France, Samuel Champlain, recognized in him the qualities of an able ambassador for advancing French interests in the New World, and Nicolet was up to the challenge. He accepted the assignment to a course of training that began with being sent to live among the Indians, to learn their language and customs. After a number of years experiencing many hardships and hunger, he became well-prepared to face the difficulties while engaging a harsh and unfamiliar wilderness as an explorer. He returned to Quebec where he was then employed as a clerk and interpreter for the next two years.

Like many diplomatic leaders of the time, Champlain was eager to discover a short route to India and the Orient; finding it would mean honor and glory for himself and for France.

But it would be a daring mission for any explorer, amidst the warring Indian tribes known to populate the west. Nicolet's first objective was to negotiate peace among the tribes. Then he was to penetrate westward as far as possible in an attempt to discover the passage to China.

With a less-than-accurate map, Nicolet set out westward in a canoe in July, 1634. From Montreal he followed the Ottawa River to Lake Nipissing, then down the French River to Georgian Bay, where he stopped to rest with the Hurons.

His journey continued westward until he reached the Sault Ste. Marie, the waterway connecting Lake Huron and Lake Superior, and then without investigating Lake Superior he turned southward, passing through the Straits of Mackinac. He paddled along the northern shore of Lake Michigan to the mouth of the Menominee River. An Algonquin tribe there told him about "Men of the Sea" not far distant. Nicolet jumped to the conclusion that he had almost reached China.

Donned in an elegant Oriental robe, he pressed on to the head of the bay, intending to impress the people of China. When he arrived, however, he was met by a band of Winnebago Indians whose language he didn't understand. Greatly disappointed—and perhaps embarrassed—that he had not discovered the China shore, Nicolet proceeded, though, to negotiate a peace agreement between the Winnebago and Huron tribes, and urged them to transport their furs to Montreal to trade for the white man's goods. The negotiations were a success, and the occasion was celebrated with a great feast of wild game.

Nicolet continued his expedition southward on the Fox River to Lake Winnebago, and then on to a Mascoutin Indian village at approximately the site of present-day Berlin in Green Lake County. Although he heard this tribe talk about the Mississippi River, he failed to recognize its importance.

Instead of continuing his journey westward, he chose to travel south where he visited with the Illinois tribes, and then returned to the Fox River and Green Bay.

About one year after he had begun, Nicolet returned to Montreal in July 1635 without ever seeing the Mighty Mississippi River.

Twenty years later, two more Frenchmen arrived in the Green Bay territory. Pierre Radisson and Menard Groseilliers remained for two years. They, too, visited with several native tribes—the Ottawa, Mascoutin, and Pottawatomi—but they went no farther west than Nicolet had been. It is likely that their intensions were not necessarily focused on exploration, but rather to establish trading relation with the natives, as in 1659 they started out on another voyage that followed Nicolet's earlier route to Sault Ste. Marie, and then westward to Lake Superior, where, on Chequamegon Bay they built a small fort and entered into friendly relations with the Hurons.

Radisson and Groseilliers joined the Hurons for the winter hunt, however, deep snow and harsh weather prevented much success, and a period of famine resulted in 500 or more deaths from starvation among the natives. The two French voyagers narrowly escaped the same fate, managing to survive by eating tree bark until the weather allowed them to attain a small supply of game. Further wanderings took them into Sioux country across the St. Croix River.

The governor of New France (Canada) was not in favor of their expedition, and when they returned to Montreal in August 1660, their more than 300 beaver pelts were confiscated. Naturally, they were so angered by this, that they offered their services to the English. Eventually, King Charles II granted a charter for the Hudson Bay Fur Company, and the French lost the splendid fur trade of a vast region.

The French, however, continued to apply their influence in the land that would become Wisconsin. To further their relations with the natives, missionaries were sent to convert the Indians to peaceful, God-fearing people. Father Rene Menard, a Jesuit, came with a returning party of trading Indians in 1660. They abandoned him on the shores of Keweenaw Bay, and after a deplorable winter, with only one companion he started out to re-join the Huron fugitives, former members of the Ontario mission; they were thought to be occupying the region that was the headwaters of the Black River. During his journey down the Wisconsin River in a small craft, Father Menard was lost at one of the upper river portages. Whether he was killed by beast or native is not absolutely certain, but because his cassock and kettle were later found in a Sioux lodge, it is likely that he was murdered.

Five years later, Father Claude Allouez was sent to continue the work of Father Menard. Although he suffered many hardships in his efforts, he was a man of determination. At Chequamegon Bay— near the present city of Ashland—he constructed a rudimentary chapel, the first Christian church erected in Wisconsin, and for two years he taught religion to natives from the entire Wisconsin territory. Then in 1669 he moved to the area of Green Bay. There he established missions along the bay shore, and in the Fox and Wolf River valleys among the Menominee, Pottawatomi, Sauk, Fox, Miami, Mascoutin, and Kickapoo native tribes. Father Allouez and his fellow workers built the first permanent Wisconsin mission—At. Francis Xavier established in 1671—at the DePere rapids on the Fox River.

That same year, the king of France, Louis XIV, declared possession of all this western country for the French sovereignty. He enlisted Nicholas Perrot, a notable fur trader and explorer of the territory since 1665, to assemble the chiefs of the Wisconsin native tribes to attend a ceremony on the western shore of Sault Ste. Marie, in recognition of this great occasion. They watched in awe as priests and warriors chanted praise of God and of the French King, and made the declaration that all the Indians' country west of Lake Michigan was annexed to the French domain, and that all natives of this land were, from that day forward, subjects of a foreign monarch.

The French leader sent yet another pair of explorers on an expedition to seek a water passage route to the Orient. It was still unknown that a vast continent stretched 2,000 miles before them. Father Jacques Marquette (a Jesuit Priest) and Louis Jolliet, (priest turned fur trader) reached the Mississippi via the Fox River, Lake Winnebago, and the Wisconsin River by June 1673, making them the first to navigate the full distance of the Wisconsin. Their journey provided the first official information about the entire territory, and marked the beginning of French control of the land that remained until the end of the French and Indian War in 1763.

A few years later, Nicholas Perrot was installed as Governor-General of the new French territory west of Lake Michigan. He established a number of trading posts, most of them along the Upper Mississippi River. It was at Fort St. Antoine on the east bank of Lake Pepin in 1689 that Perrot declared for France the possession of the Sioux territory, and he was the first European to discover and explore the lead mine region of southwestern Wisconsin.

Little was known about the Wisconsin territory by the people of the English colonies on the Atlantic coast, or by anyone except the French until 1778 when Capt. Jonathan Carver of Connecticut published his book of travels through the region, which he had done twelve years before. He had visited the Green Bay settlement (then called Fort Edward Augustus, where there were a few French families) and then went on to visit a large Winnebago community at the entrance of Lake Winnebago. His travels took him to Prairie du Chien via the Fox and Wisconsin Rivers, stopping along the way at a village of the Sacs near the site of present-day Prairie du Sac, and at a village of Fox near present-day Muscoda. From Prairie du Chien, his expedition continued up the Mississippi to Lake Pepin. During his exploration in what would become Minnesota, he spent several months among the Sioux, and after his return to civilization, he claimed that he had been given a grant by the Sioux of some 14,000 square miles of lands in the Mississippi River Valley. In later years, his descendants attempted to establish claims on that land, however, the claims were denied by Congress.

THE FUR TRADING ERA

Fur pelts from deer, elk, bear, and especially beaver were in high demand in Europe, and the French had cornered the market with their new-found source in the land of Wisconsin with its numerous lakes, rivers, and eager cooperation of the Native American hunters and trappers.

But the British had muscled their way into the fur trade, and conflicts erupted over the control of the land as well as the fur trade. After years of conflicts that culminated in the French and Indian War, the British finally won. The Treaty of Paris ceded all of Canada and the land that France claimed along the Mississippi River to the British, and they relinquished their fur trading empire as well.

The French fur trade had introduced the first European influence to Wisconsin, and as the British gained control, not much changed. The region remained sparsely settled, except for the Native Americans and the traders. Few Europeans wanted to settle in the midst of harsh winters and frequent Indian conflicts. But many of the traders actually lived with the Indians and took Indian wives. It was a dangerous lifestyle if they attempted to settle on their own, as there was yet no government or any form of protection from Indian uprisings.

The British did make some changes to the fur trade, however. Furs were now sent to London instead of Paris. British investors brought about the increase in size of the trading companies and spread them farther into the northwest as the beaver population dwindled. This growth of large trade companies reduced the power of the Native tribes. The British managed to maintain control of the fur trade after the American Revolution, but then they were finally forced out after the War of 1812.

By the time Americans had complete control of the trade, it was unfortunately in serious decline. Tremendous reduction of the beaver population and the removal of the Native Americans to reservations combined to devastate the fur trade in the Wisconsin Territory. Traders were now moving their operations to the untouched Pacific Northwest where fur-bearing wildlife was still bountiful. Wisconsin had served as successful trading headquarters for the French, British, and Americans for nearly 200 years, but now the decline in the fur trade allowed the territory to shift from a frontier wilderness to a settled civilization.

THE AMERICAN REVOLUTION
and the WAR OF 1812

Not many Americans lived in the Wisconsin region, nor was Wisconsin a part of the United States at the time of the American Revolution, so it was little affected by the war. American victory did little to change the area; French and British traders still remained scattered throughout the region, and even though all the trading posts were in American hands twenty years later, the British still continued to control the trade from Canada.

Only after another war with England, the War of 1812, did the Americans take control of the fur trade. Following the American victory, the American flag was finally raised on Wisconsin soil, and the Wisconsin Territory was officially part of the United States.

WISCONSIN NATIVES

The territory now known as Wisconsin became home to many Native American tribes long before any European explorers arrived. Although many of these tribe names are familiar to us today as "Wisconsin" tribes, most of them did not originate there, but rather migrated to the region from various other locations. And because these earliest people who populated Wisconsin Territory had no written language to record their migration travels, only the artifacts they left behind are our clues to determine their presence, their cultural traits, and movement patterns. Extensive archaeological studies have uncovered some very surprising facts regarding the presence of human habitation in various Wisconsin areas—some widespread, and some isolated.

AZTALAN

It is safe to say that Aztalan was the first farming community in the state of Wisconsin, and perhaps the first ghost town.

A thousand years ago Wisconsin was inhabited mostly by wild creatures. However, there did exist at that time people of an advanced culture. When evidence of their earlier presence in Wisconsin was first discovered in 1836 by a settler at a location about 50 miles west of the new village of Milwaukee, little was known about the long since vanished civilization. But the flat-topped pyramid-like mounds found there were definitely man-made, and soon became a great curiosity and subject of broad study.

The name Aztalan was given to the site of an apparent village by Judge Nathaniel Hyer, an early resident of Milwaukee. Reports of the ruins of an ancient walled city had reached Milwaukee, and from the description, Hyer took great interest in seeing it for himself. He traveled on horseback to the site in 1836, and again in 1837 to draw the first map of the area. His narrative description and map were published in Chicago and Milwaukee newspapers. He compared his observations with reports he had read about the Aztecs in Mexico, who also built similar pyramids of stone. Their traditional lore told of ancestors coming from a land they called Aztalan, a place in the distant north. Hyer jumped to the conclusion that this was that place, and incorrectly named the site Aztalan. At first, his assumption was accepted, and the name remained.

Investigation of this band of people would eventually reveal that they mysteriously abandoned the village and disappeared from Wisconsin about AD 1250. They were of the Mississippian Culture, and are believed to have migrated north to Wisconsin after the last ice sheet had disappeared and had been replaced by vegetation. These people came from Cahokia, another ancient city located across the Mississippi River from present-day St. Louis, Missouri. Aztalan's direct connection with Cahokia is apparent in the likeness of mound construction and cultural traits revealed by thousands of artifacts that have been uncovered.

The site of Aztalan developed into the largest and most significant archaeological survey in the state of Wisconsin. In a century and a half of intense study, the thousands of artifacts recovered from the site have aided in determining Aztalan culture. Professional archaeological excavation has revealed much evidence as to paint a fairly accurate picture of the ancient city, and has helped us to better understand what Aztalan was and who built it.

Increase A. Lapham, considered as Wisconsin's first scientist, also made a study of the Aztalan site and drew more detailed maps of the 21-acre village and its surrounding area in 1850. He, too, concurred with Hyer regarding the similarities with Mexican Aztec "architecture" which led him to believe this was the land of Aztalan, an important segment of Aztec lore.

It would be after the turn of the Twentieth Century when the Wisconsin Archeological Society was formally chartered (1906) and efforts were made to preserve and document the site. By that time, unfortunately, treasure seekers had severely damaged the mounds digging for relics, and farmers had plowed and planted crops on the land, all but leveling many of the visible features. Fortunately, Lapham's maps had recorded them. The myths of Aztalan's connection to the Mexican Aztecs were finally disproved. Attention was then appropriately directed to the association with the Mississippian Culture of Cahokia in Illinois.

A population of some 500 people made their homes within the walled city of Aztalan. The fortification walls surrounding the settlement were constructed of vertical timbers and then plastered with a clay and grass mixture to give the appearance of concrete. Houses were built in the same manor using thatched or bark roofs. Archaeologists have determined that the large flat-topped mounds weren't necessarily burial mounds as have been discovered elsewhere, but were built for the purpose of conducting rituals, and perhaps to place the houses of important people of the town, namely a chief and his family. Inside the enclosure, too, was a large plaza for social activities, housing sectors for the common citizens, and large underground food storage facilities. Without any doubt, this civilization was well organized and structured. Although the

Mississippian culture did not have a written language, their history and lifestyle has been pieced together through artwork left behind in the form of pottery and crafts, tools, implements, and weaponry.

Outside the fortification walls, vast fields of corn were cultivated by the Mississippian farmers. In addition they grew squash, pumpkins and sunflowers. It is safe to say that Aztalan was the first farming town in Wisconsin, hundreds of years before Europeans set foot on the soil. They were probably attracted to this region along the banks of the Crawfish River because of its abundant fish and clam, wild game, (especially deer) large flocks of waterfowl, and dense stands of wild rice. The setting was perfect with ample resources to support their population.

From the remains that have been found and studied, it is known that fire destroyed the city, but it is not certain what caused the disaster. There is some speculation that the people of Aztalan practiced cannibalism to some degree, and it is quite possible that other Indian tribes intentionally burned the town and drove its occupants away.

IN MORE RECENT TIMES...

A number of various native cultures occupied various parts of Wisconsin, but as mentioned earlier, most origins were not Wisconsin. Many came from the North American eastern seaboard; their migration to the Midwest resulted from several reasons: climate surely was a factor in some cases; depletion of food sources in their home areas caused some to seek new hunting grounds; the intrusion of Europeans drove some westward; and what seems to be the most dramatic factor was the hostile attitudes of some tribes toward others.

Of all the Native tribes that have lived in Wisconsin, only the Menominee and the Winnebago were true aboriginals whose existence in the region extends beyond human memory, possibly 5000 years. The Winnebago do not remember a time when they didn't live at Red Banks on the south shore of Green Bay. Their occupation of Wisconsin is very ancient; although they have no recollection of mound-building, they may very well be descendents of the earlier Mississippian, Hopewell, and Adena cultures. Their original homeland was the northeast

Wisconsin area between Green Bay and Lake Winnebago, but they eventually dominated most of Wisconsin from Upper Michigan to present-day Milwaukee, and west to the Mississippi River.

The Menominee's earliest known homeland was near Sault Ste. Marie and Michilimackinac. Sometime around 1400 they were forced southwest by the arrival of the Ojibwe and Potawatomi from the east. Their new homeland was along the Menominee River, present-day border between Wisconsin and Upper Michigan. Their territory extended north to Escanaba, Michigan, and south to Oconto, Wisconsin prior to the arrival of the French fur traders. Becoming quite active in the fur trade, they quickly extended their hunting region west. By 1700, the once dominating Winnebago had nearly been wiped out by war and epidemic, and the Menominee spread south and west, occupying the vacated space. At their peak, the Menominee controlled most of central Wisconsin. However, after 1832, white settlement and commercial logging rapidly reduced their available land and were eventually confined to a 235,000 acre reservation in northeast Wisconsin, where they have remained to present day.

The first Frenchman to encounter the two friendly tribes was Jean Nicollet in 1634 and again in 1639. But during the next 30 years, the relatively peaceful conditions in northern Wisconsin were disrupted. Thousands of refugees—Potawatomi, Fox, Sauk, Ottawa, Huron, Mascouten, Kickapoo, Tionontati—had been maliciously forced from their homelands in the eastern Great Lakes regions by the formidable, warring Iroquois of New York. As they fled west to avoid massacre, they relocated in northern Wisconsin and Upper Michigan. The same pressure drove the Ojibwe south and west from Sault Ste. Marie.

This enormous and sudden influx nearly destroyed the aboriginal Winnebago and Menominee. Competition for available resources had transformed Wisconsin into a place of war, epidemic, and starvation. The Sturgeon War between the Menominee and Ojibwe resulted as the Menominee placed a series of fences across the Menominee River to easily catch the sturgeon swimming upstream from Lake Michigan to spawn. The restrictions prevented any of the fish from getting into the Ojibwe territory, cutting off the much needed food supply. Warnings from the

Ojibwe were ignored, and the Ojibwe attacked and destroyed a Menominee village. Because they were too few in number, the Menominee were unable to retaliate alone, so they sought assistance from the Fox, Sauk, and Potawatomi near Green Bay, thus spreading the conflict far beyond the original opponents. At the same time, the unrelenting Iroquois warriors had pursued the fleeing eastern tribes to Michigan and Wisconsin, and were attacking and destroying anyone they encountered.

The hostile conditions in Wisconsin had resulted from a series of events long before that occurred far to the east. Knowing the warring nature of the Iroquois, the French had suppressed trade relations with them, avoiding their acquisition of firearms, but had supplied the Algonquin and Montagnais with weapons. These tribes were then able to drive the Iroquois from the St. Lawrence Valley in 1610. The Dutch, however, were more interested in the profits of trade than in keeping peace, and the Iroquois soon entered into trade relations with the Dutch along the Hudson River. By 1645 the Iroquois had taken control of the lower Ottawa Valley, blocked access to the western Great Lakes, and brought the

French fur trade to a halt. With so few Frenchmen in North America at the time, they had no choice but to make peace with the Iroquois, forcing them to remain neutral while the Iroquois attacked and destroyed the Huron in 1649. Within the next three years, other French allies suffered a similar fate.

For a few years, the French maintained the truce with the Iroquois, and encouraged what remained of their allies to deliver furs to Montreal. The Ottawa, Huron and Ojibwe formed large canoe fleets to force their way past Iroquois war parties on the Ottawa River. The Iroquois retaliated by attacking the refugee villages in Wisconsin.

Encouraged immigration had greatly increased French population in Canada; now they were better able to resist the Iroquois aggression and soon ended the peace agreement. A regiment of French soldiers began a series of attacks on villages in the Iroquois homeland in 1664. The French then resumed travel and trade in the western Great Lakes region.

A year later, fur trader Nicolas Perrot, Jesuit Claude-Jean Allouez, and other Frenchmen accompanied a large Huron and Ottawa trading party on its return journey from Montreal. They fought their way past the Ottawa Valley Iroquois and arrived at Green Bay just at the approach of winter; this was the first French appearance in the area since Nicolet in 1634. But there had been a drastic population reduction in the original Wisconsin tribes. The Menominee and Winnebago had nearly been exterminated, with less than 400 Menominee and only a remnant of the once dominant Winnebago remaining. War and epidemic had created the chaotic conditions that lingered until 1667 when the French finally gained the upper hand on the Iroquois.

The peace lasted thirteen years, allowing the French to resume their fur trade, and to bring stability to the region. Perrot established a trading post at Green Bay, and missionaries followed a couple of years later. Although the Jesuits visited the Menominee, most of their efforts were concentrated on the Huron and Ottawa, with whom they had enjoyed some earlier successful converts. The Menominee kept their traditional religion for the time being, but trade was another issue, as the Menominee underwent a fundamental economic change and became hunters for profit. Competition for hunting territory might have added to an already tense situation, but the French used their influence to terminate much of the warfare; it interfered with the fur trade. Nicolas Perrot understood native peoples well and began to mediate the intertribal disputes near Green Bay, benefitting all parties and allowing the French trade to expand.

Although the French fur trade caused much of their troubles, it also saved the Menominee and Winnebago from extinction by restricting warfare and mediating the disputes, but some serious problems remained. Perrot was able to reconcile a Fox-Ojibwe war, and Daniel Dulhut arranged a peace between the Ojibwe and Dakota, there was still friction in the region due to crowding which the French could never resolve completely. They never achieved a satisfactory relationship with the Fox, and the ever-present hostility between the Ojibwe and Dakota periodically erupted into confrontations for hunting territory along the southern shore of Lake Superior.

The peace in the western Great Lakes region came to a violent end in 1680 with yet another Iroquois attack against the Illinois. However, the unity that had evolved during the period of peace prevailed; the Iroquois could no longer have their way in the west without serious opposition.

The Iroquois failure to conquer Fort St. Louis on the upper Illinois River in 1684 was the turning point in the Beaver Wars. The French began to organize and arm the Algonquin. Taking the offensive in 1687, the alliance had to Iroquois on the run back towards New York. The war finally concluded with a peace treaty signed in 1701, leaving the French and their allies in control of the Great Lakes. Unfortunately, the timing of this victory coincided with an overabundance of beaver fur on the European market. Prices dropped sharply. In addition, Jesuit protest about the corruption that the fur trade had created among Native Americans influenced the decision by the French crown to suspend fur trade in the western Great Lakes region. The trading post at Green Bay closed, taking the Menominee temporarily out of the fur trade.

The defeated Iroquois were quick to take advantage of the opportunity to weaken the French by offering their native allies access to the British traders at Albany. As a rule, British goods were of better quality and at a lower price. The ploy was a success, and the French alliance soon fell apart. In desperation, the French in Canada convinced Paris to permit the establishment of a new post at Detroit for trade with the Great Lakes tribes in 1701. Virtually every tribe moved to the vicinity of the new post, with the exception of the Menominee and Winnebago who remained in Wisconsin. Their small population had played no part in the French and Algonquin victory over the Iroquois, and they were too far west for the offers of British trade goods. They had no intentions of leaving their homeland to settle near Fort Pontchartrain at Detroit.

This turn of events was beneficial to the Menominee; the refugee tribes began leaving northern Wisconsin. Relations with the Dakota and Ojibwe remained friendly, and they could once again hunt, fish, and gather wild rice with a certain amount of peace and security. Slowly, the Menominee population began to recover.

Tension at Fort Pontchartrain caused by overcrowding by too many tribes resulted in conflict; the French were attacked by Fox, Mascouten, and Kickapoo. Other French allies rushed in to assist; a great slaughter followed, and the Fox and their allies were forced back to Wisconsin where they continued to attack the French and their allies.

The Fox Wars were civil wars between

members of the Great Lakes alliance, and they must have been certain satisfaction to the Iroquois and British. The Menominee remained neutral during the first Fox War. Fighting ended in 1716, but the Fox continued to antagonize the French with their constant confrontations with the Illinois and Osage. As the Fox acquired other native allies to fight these enemies, the French began to suspect a threat, and decided to destroy the Fox. They isolated the Fox from potential allies, and after convincing the Winnebago and Dakota to switch sides, they attacked the Fox in 1728. This time, the Menominee were involved; they refused Fox alliance and joined the French. A combined Winnebago, Menominee, Ojibwe war party attacked a Fox hunting village, killing at least 80 warriors and capturing some 70 women and children.

Meanwhile, the French had reoccupied their old fort at Green Bay. Concerned about possible retaliation from the Fox, the Winnebago moved closer to Green Bay and built a fortified village on an island in the Fox River. Their enemy soon found them, but the fortification was too strong for an effective attack, so they waited for an opportunity.

At Green Bay, the French commander heard of

the battle and set out with French militia and Menominee warriors. The Fox finally abandoned the siege.

This second Fox War turned even uglier when, in 1730, most of the Fox decided to flee east to join the Iroquois. But the French and their allies caught up with them in northern Illinois. During that battle, the Fox were almost annihilated; a few survivors found refuge with the Sauk near Green Bay. A French expedition followed them to the village and demanded their surrender. When the Sauk refused, another battle ensued, and the French commander was killed. As the French retreated to regroup, the Sauk and Fox took this opportunity to abandon their village and fled west. They crossed the Mississippi River and settled in Iowa. The following year, another French expedition, accompanied by Menominee warriors, was sent there to seek and destroy the Sauk and Fox in their new refuge. This effort also failed.

By this time, the French allies were becoming alarmed with the idea of genocide. At a conference in Montreal, the Menominee and Winnebago asked the French to show mercy to the Fox, while the Potawatomi and Ottawa made the same request on behalf of the Sauk. Because they were confronted by new conflicts with the Dakota in the west and the Chickasaw in the south, the French reluctantly agreed to a peace with the Fox and Sauk. Despite their efforts to stop the French from completely destroying them, the Fox and Sauk never forgave the Menominee for their participation in the second Fox War; a lasting hostility had been created.

The Menominee, though, were at peace with almost every other tribe in the region. Following the Fox Wars, their alliance with the French was even stronger. Their numbers had increased while the population of others had fallen, and they began to expand southwestward into central Wisconsin areas recently vacated by the Sauk and Fox. Although the neighboring Ojibwe and Dakota were bitter enemies to each other, neither tribe objected to the Menominee movement. The Menominee maintained friendly relations with both; they could hunt freely in territory where Dakota and Ojibwe warriors would kill each other when they met. Only the Fox and Sauk remained a threat.

The Menominee and Winnebago joined with other tribes to aid the French in protecting Quebec from British invasion, although the Menominee contribution to the war effort was minimal. They were also involved in other conflicts, allied with Ojibwe, Potawatomi and Mascouten against the Peoria in1746, and with the Winnebago in a separate war west of the Mississippi River against the Missouri. The pattern of limited participation by the Menominee continued in the last major conflict between Britain and France for the control of North America—the French and Indian War of 1755-63. But that participation came at a price: while fighting in the east, the Great Lakes warriors contracted smallpox in 1757 and brought it back to their homeland villages that winter. The resulting epidemic left the Menominee with only 800 people, and combined with fewer trade goods put a strain on their French loyalty. As the war turned against them, the French grew arrogant and abusive, and a Menominee uprising at Green Bay killed 22 French soldiers. The Menominee soon regretted their actions, as members of the war party were later captured and sent to Montreal for punishment; several were executed.

But the capture of Quebec by the British ended the French reign in North America. Montreal surrendered the next year, and by 1761, British soldiers occupied Green Bay. The breakdown of French authority in the region had brought the

Winnebago, Menominee, and Potawatomi at Green Bay to the verge of war with the Michilimackinac Ojibwe, but the British assumed the old French practice of mediating and providing trade goods. Preventing the outbreak of serious warfare, the British won the trust and loyalty of the Winnebago and Menominee. During the next 50 years, the Winnebago and Menominee would ally with the British, fighting both the Spanish and Americans during the Revolutionary War and the War of 1812.

After the War of 1812, settlement began to advance up the Mississippi from St. Louis, but warfare in Iowa and Minnesota between the Dakota, Ojibwe, Fox, and Sauk slowed its progress. The government attempted to end the fighting in 1825 at a grand council held with the area's tribes at Prairie du Chien. Attended by the Ojibwe, Fox, Sauk, Menominee, Iowa, Sioux, Winnebago, Ottawa, and Potawatomi, the resulting treaty established boundaries between them. It also created a 40-mile wide buffer zone between the Dakota, Fox and Sauk in northeast Iowa. Called the Neutral Ground, the Americans hoped to relocate the Winnebago there since they were friendly with both sides, but the Winnebago did not favor this arrangement.

Since its purpose was to smooth the progress of settlement, the treaty made almost no provisions to protect native lands from white encroachment. It had only little success in preventing warfare, but settlement afterwards moved northward at an accelerated pace. During the next fifteen years, the Winnebago were forced to surrender most of their homeland. Miners rushed in to claim the rich lead deposits in northwestern Illinois and southwestern Wisconsin, and nothing was done by the government to prevent encroachment. Less than two years after a treaty was signed at Prairie du Chien, the Winnebago declared war to defend their territory. Led by the Winnebago Prophet White Cloud and the war chief Red Bird, fighting began in the summer of 1827 when a barge ascending the Mississippi near Prairie du Chien was fired upon. Other attacks killed some settlers along the lower Wisconsin River and struck the lead mines near Galena, Illinois. Soldiers were rushed north from St. Louis, and by August it was over. Faced with a war they could not win, Red Bird and White Cloud surrendered. Red Bird died in prison, but White Cloud was pardoned by the president and was released. Meanwhile, in a treaty signed at Green Bay in August, 1828, the

Winnebago, Ojibwe, Potawatomi, and Ottawa ceded northern Illinois for $540,000.

The last serious conflict between Americans and the natives in Wisconsin came in 1832. Blackhawk's Sauk tribe at Rock Island, Illinois refused to relinquish their land, but after the Menominee and Dakota murdered fifteen Fox chiefs enroute to a meeting with the Americans at Prairie du Chien, war seemed eminent. Blackhawk brought his people west into Iowa to protect the Fox and Sauk villages there from the Dakota attacks which never came. When he started back to Illinois, the Americans refused to allow him to cross the Mississippi.

In the spring of 1832, the chief defiantly led his people back across the Mississippi to reclaim their former territory, convinced that the British and other native tribes would join him against the Americans. This was the first act that touched off the Blackhawk War. The anticipated help did not materialize; pursued by the army and Illinois militia, Blackhawk retreated towards Wisconsin hoping to reach safety among either the Winnebago or Ojibwe. But most Winnebago wanted nothing to do with him and refused to help. After several confrontations, Blackhawk realized that he no longer had friends among the other native tribes. He turned his people westward in an attempt to return to Iowa, but they never made it. Trapped between an American army and gunboat at the mouth of the Bad Axe River, the Sauk were slaughtered before surrendering. Menominee and Dakota warriors killed many of those who managed to elude capture by the Americans.

Chief Blackhawk, however, escaped before the battle and fled north. He was captured by the Winnebago Chief Choukeka, a friend of the Americans, who delivered him to the Indian Agent at Prairie du Chien.

The Winnebago ceded their land east of the Mississippi in a harsh treaty negotiated by General Winfield Scott at Fort Armstrong in September, 1832, and agreed to move to Neutral Ground in northeast Iowa. Over the next four decades they were moved and removed many times to locations in Minnesota, South Dakota, and Nebraska. Some had managed to stay in Wisconsin, but were routinely being arrested and transported to the Nebraska reservation. Within a month, they were usually back in Wisconsin. After ten years of this game, the government finally gave up and purchased homestead lands for the Winnebago, and let them stay. During the 1880s, over half of the Nebraska Winnebago came home to Wisconsin where they have remained every since, scattered across ten counties.

As for the Menominee, a final treaty signed with the United States in 1856 ceded two townships for the purpose of creating a reservation. This reservation included 235,000 acres of their homeland. Joined later by a small group of Potawatomi, the Menominee have remained in this location ever since. But it wasn't always as easy as it sounds; timber interests in northern Wisconsin became the focal point of wealth seekers, and it was soon observed that the government had made an error by giving this valuable White Pine timberland to the Menominee. Every known dishonest means was attempted to relieve the tribe of the 350 square miles of prime forest, but all efforts failed. Under government supervision, the Menominee began operation of their own tribally-owned and operated sawmill in 1872 which competed with all other private lumber companies in the area. Wisconsin's timber was soon depleted, and the many lumber barons moved on, but the Menominee remained. They began a program of sustained yield harvest in

1908, the first large scale application of this concept in the United States. Designed to assure an income for future generations, it was a great success, and the lumber industry remained the primary source of income for the Menominee.

The Federal Government terminated the Menominee's tribal status in 1961, and their reservation became a Wisconsin county. The sawmill could no longer provide enough tax base to pay for all the services a county government was required to provide, and the Menominee instantly went from being one of the most self-sufficient tribes in the United States to the lowest standard of living in Wisconsin. To meet their obligations, the Menominee were forced to sell part of their reservation as lakefront lots for vacation homes. Federal recognition was restored in 1973.

DOOR COUNTY FORTRESS

Just up the coastline from Jacksonport in Door County, Hibbard Creek rambles through lowland on its way from the rocky inlands of the peninsula to gently wash over a sandbar into the big waters of Lake Michigan. It was there that the great village of the Potawatomi—Mechingan— once stood on the banks of Hibbard Creek.

Mechingan was established following a ten-year war in which the Potawatomi subdued the Winnebago, forcing them to move southwestward to the shores of the big inland lake that now bears their name.

Then came a period of tranquility on the peninsula, however, it was not to last long. Another less-peace-loving eastern tribe, the Iroquois, would soon pose a serious threat, and tranquil Door Peninsula would become a battle ground.

The Potawatomi came from the northeast with the Ottawa and Ojibwa to the eastern shore of Lake Huron, probably around 1400 after the North American climate became colder. They eventually settled in the northern portion of lower Michigan. By then, the three tribes were separated, but there still remained the memory of their close alliance.

Their move to the west side of Lake Michigan occurred around 1630 when the Huron, Ottawa, and Tionontati had exhausted the beaver in their homelands and were forcefully seizing new hunting territory from the tribes in lower Michigan. It is unlikely that Jean Nicollet encountered the Potawatomi on his 1634 exploration of Wisconsin, as he followed the northern shore of Lake Michigan while enroute to Green Bay.

Because the Iroquois of New York were perhaps the most savage and vicious of all Indians, the French had carefully avoided selling arms and ammunition to them. But the Dutch did not practice such caution, as they were more interested in trade profits than preventing bloodshed. As soon as they had acquired the Dutch arms, they announced their intentions of exterminating their neighbors—red and white— for as far as they might travel in all directions. In just a few years they had destroyed countless Indian villages and had accumulated more than 50,000 scalps.

Tribes who were friendly to the whites, particularly the French, suffered the most. Without guns, they could not defend themselves against the Iroquois, and their only option was to flee westward. Some came to Green Bay, some stopped on Washington Island, and some followed a route around the south shore of Lake Michigan and did not rest until they reached central Wisconsin.

The Huron, who had stopped on Washington Island, just off the tip of the Door Peninsula, realized they were not completely safe there. Scouts had been sent back to spy on the Iroquois. When the first scouts returned in 1652, they brought only bad news: 800 Iroquois warriors were on their way with orders to track down the Huron and wipe them out. After that, they would destroy the French, and extend their predominance from the Atlantic to the Great Lakes.

Needless to say, panic was among the Huron people. They were unable to defend themselves, and evading the blood-thirsty Iroquois seemed futile. So with the Ottawa, they sent a delegation down to Mechingan in hopes that their Potawatomi friends would help them. In larger number, all of them together might be able to stand off the Iroquois, and perhaps, with the grace of the Great Spirit, be victorious over them.

The Potawatomi villagers showed passion for their allies and agreed to allow the refugees protection at Mechingan; within a few weeks, the population there rose from 1,500 to over 4,000.

Almost a year passed without any sign of the attackers. But the relentless Iroquois continued searching blindly through the strange country.

Mechingan was crowded, but with a triple stockade of stout timbers surrounding the village, it was secure. For months hunters had been bringing in deer, beaver, and fish. Maize and other vegetables had been harvested and carefully stored. The people were nervous, as the Iroquois were expected at any time, but they felt reasonably safe. No one ventured very far beyond the village walls.

The Iroquois warriors did arrive, not expecting to find such a fortress that would not be easily penetrated. They were probably astonished at the sight, with thoughts that no village had ever held out long against them. But Mechingan and its inhabitants presented a new challenge. The Iroquois may have attempted an attack, but quickly learned that it was useless and a waste of ammunition. So they settled in to plan their siege.

As proficient as they were in battle, the Iroquois were alarmingly poor at hunting. Game in the surrounding forest was now scarce due to the skills of the Potawatomi, and the fish were nearly impossible to catch. The warriors had carried some corn with them on their long expedition, but it was gone.

Choosing humility over starvation, the invincible Iroquois agreed to release their prisoners and meekly asked for peace. The people of Mechingan graciously accepted the proposition, and promised that every member of the Iroquois war party would be given a corn cake upon leaving the country.

The generous offer to provide their enemies with all that precious food, however, was not exactly a simple gesture of forgiveness; the Huron and Ottawa had been chased by the Iroquois far too long to only call the whole thing even. They poisoned every cake, and every Iroquois warrior might have died in agony. But when the cakes were tossed over the stockade walls, the chief ordered them to be left untouched. He picked up one and fed it to a hungry dog. Within a few minutes, the dog fell dead.

If the mighty Iroquois were humiliated when they were forced by hunger to seek a peaceful conclusion, now they lost all dignity. Silently they packed up and left. Some went north, only to fall into a trap set by the Ojibwa and were nearly destroyed. The others went south into Illinois country where the Illinois met them with such force as to nearly wipe them out. Only a few stragglers eventually made it back to New York. The Iroquois rampage was over, and peace on the Door Peninsula resumed.

THE PIONEER VILLAGES

AZTALAN

Several hundred years after the demise of the ancient Indian village, a small but thriving pioneer village blossomed adjacent to the "Ancient City" ruins when the Wisconsin Territory had not yet become a state. As the site of the old town had been given the name Aztalan by surveyor Nathaniel Hyer, the name carried over to the new settlement. Located at a busy junction of two Territorial Roads—the Milwaukee to Mineral Point Road, and the stagecoach road between Janesville and Fond du Lac—Aztalan flourished and grew from the first log house of Thomas Brayton, and by 1842 when it became the first incorporated village in Jefferson County, it was the leading business and industrial center in that county with hotels, blacksmith shops, a wagon builder, shoe shop, fanning mill, brickyard, a saleratus factory, three stores, a steam operated sawmill, tree nursery, and stone quarry.

Aztalan was the site of Jefferson County's first Post Office in 1837, with Nathaniel Hyer as Postmaster. Originally named Jefferson, this Post Office became known as Aztalan within two years, and it operated until 1904 when it was closed as a result of Rural Free Delivery.

Transportation was a key factor in the success of any pioneer town. Aztalan enjoyed the prosperity stemming from the traffic of two busy thoroughfares crossing the state, maintaining the community's liveliness. But then the age of the railroad came—or more accurately, *didn't come* to Aztalan. The Northwestern tracks missed the town by five miles in 1859. Soon to follow, the traffic on the roads passing through Aztalan diminished as a result of the growing popularity of railroad freight and passenger movement. Two more railroads bypassed the village in 1881 and '82, only by a mile, yet too far away to be an effective asset. The village of Aztalan began fading, and by the turn of the century, it was no more than a ghost town at a quiet crossroad. All that remained by 1912 was the Baptist Church, a creamery, and a general store that had doubled as the last Post Office before Rural Free Delivery. Church services were held for only a year or two longer, and the store burned down in 1925.

Revival did come to Aztalan, though, in 1941 when the Lake Mills-Aztalan Historical Society was founded. The Society took over the old, decaying church, and in a monumental effort restored the only remaining original building and opened its museum with fascinating displays of Indian artifacts and pioneer relics. More recently, the pioneer settlement has been recreated with authentic log cabins and an original Moravian log church that were moved to the site from other nearby locations.

NESHONOC

Monroe Palmer, a millwright and speculator, came to La Crosse County from Vermont in 1851, purchased fifteen acres of land on the La Crosse River and constructed a dam and sturdy grist mill with hand hewed oak timbers. His mill eventually began furnishing large quantities of feed and flour to the many logging camps in the general area. Three years later, he hired a surveyor to plat a village he called "Neshonoc," after the Indian name for the area. The only post office between La Crosse and Sparta was established there. Mail was carried on foot from La Crosse, but by 1853, a stagecoach delivered it three times a week. Viewed as a location with the advantage of good waterpower created by the dam, the settlement grew with more businesses, churches, a school, and homes. Many people believed that the village was destined for further growth and would become an important commercial center because of this advantage. Neshonoc was considered for the La Crosse County seat, and with the anticipated railroad near in the future, it was expected to become the site for a Milwaukee & La Crosse rail station.

Land donated to the railroad company at the site that is now West Salem became the station site in 1858, however, and because of the dominance of the transportation availability, more people settled at West Salem and more businesses established there. It was only a mile from the thriving village of Neshonoc, but with the lack of direct shipping and transportation facilities, the little village of Neshonoc could not compete with its neighbor. Its residents began moving their homes and businesses nearer the railroad. Palmer finally sold the mill, and it later burned down, but was rebuilt with limestone by its then current owner, Samuel McMillan. By the 1890s Neshonoc had all but disappeared; only the stone gristmill and dam remained.

DEKORRA

Seven miles downstream from Portage, the thriving little village of Dekorra once occupied the bank of the Wisconsin River. It was there that the first gristmill of the area was built in 1843. No other mills at the time meant a busy place, as farmers hauled their grain as far as forty miles to be processed there.

Dekorra, named after a Winnebago Indian Chief, was platted in 1837 under the direction of Thompson, Trimble & Morton, and it was they who started the construction of the mill. Others soon followed and the town quickly developed with the addition of two hotels, a post office, blacksmith, general stores, shoe shop, and the barrooms considered necessary for every river town.

Lumber rafting on the Wisconsin River played a large part in making Dekorra the successful place it was. An endless procession of rafts passed by, and the hospitable little milling town became a favorite stop for the rafters. Ox teams hauled a considerable amount of lumber to inland points from the Dekorra landing, and the taverns and barrooms offered a good place for the lumbermen to spend their money before continuing the journey down the river.

The gristmill changed ownership many times over the years, but remained a cornerstone of the community. At peak times, the mill produced as much as 250 barrels of flour per day, and shipped its product by the carload to the logging camps of the northern pineries.

Crossing the river in the early times was by means of a pole ferry. It always proved exciting, and perhaps uncertain, as one could never be exactly sure just where the landing on the opposite shore might be. Eventually, though, a cable ferry was implemented, and a river crossing could be done with a better degree of certainty.

Shortly after the Civil War began, Captain William Ryan organized the Dekorra Home Guard consisting of 100 local men. When the time for the call to duty came, the Guard was not taken as an entire organization, but instead, Capt. Ryan with about half the men joined the Iron Brigade, and the remainder went with various other outfits.

After the war, business revival followed the railroads. Lumber rafting on the Wisconsin diminished. As Dekorra's population gradually slipped away to Portage and Baraboo, the lack of patronage caused the stores and shops to close, one by one. The post office was closed, and the mill stopped its wheels forever. Sadly, Dekorra's dot on the map as a thriving pioneer metropolis is only a memory. Today, it remains as a residential community with many beautiful homes and cottages occupying the Wisconsin River banks where once the shouts of the red-shirted log rafters could be heard echoing between the hills.

HELENA

There was a day when the red-shirted raftsmen floated by on their rafts of lumber, and loaded wagons drawn by ox teams rumbled through the streets of a town named Helena just across the Wisconsin River from Spring Green. Not far away was the neighboring community of Wyoming.

The most prominent feature of Helena was the shot tower, and though it did not make Helena, neither did Helena determine the location of the shot tower.

Missouri towers had controlled the entire output of the southwestern Wisconsin mining territory. All the lead was sold at Galena and St. Louis, made into shot, and shipped down the Mississippi to the Gulf, and on to the New York markets. But Green Bay merchant, trader, and river man, Daniel Whitney saw an opportunity in 1831 for making lead shot, and he had a plan for a cheaper method of reaching the eastern markets. He selected a high bluff along the Wisconsin River to build the tower. The location was in near proximity of the mining district, and the river afforded a natural shipping avenue.

In his employ at his trading establishment at the portage of the Wisconsin and Fox Rivers was John Metcalf, who had previous experience in the Missouri shot towers. He would be put in charge of building and running Whitney's facility.

The small village of Helena already existed near the site when work on the tower began. General Dodge had laid it out, and its location on the river was expected to rival Galena. But so far, after three years, Helena consisted of only a few log huts, a tavern, and a blockhouse – one of the forts ordered by Gen. Dodge to protect the people in case of Indian trouble.

Before the tower was completed, the Black Hawk War in 1832 all but wiped out the town. Military troops demolished the houses, using the timbers to make rafts on which they pursued the fleeing Indian tribe. The blockhouse was the only structure left.

After the war, work continued. Although the original Helena residents had left, Whitney established a store and a house to accommodate his men, and in 1833 the tower was completed and in running order with six men employed. Not much shot was produced at first. Lead was hauled from Galena, and the finished shot was hauled back to Galena, primarily in exchange for supplies.

In a year's time, the town, once again, showed considerable growth – a new store, cooper shop, blacksmith shop, barracks for the men and a warehouse. Then in 1836, the tower was sold to a Buffalo, N.Y. concern, though Daniel Whitney stayed on as a part of the company. The name was changed from the Wisconsin Shot Company to the

Wisconsin Mineral and Transportation Company. Within a couple more years, Helena was a thriving town.

Alva Culver had previously worked as a carpenter on the company buildings. He rafted timber down the Wisconsin from the northern pineries to Helena and built the warehouse. Then in 1839, he returned and built his own hotel. It was the first and largest in Helena – two stories with fourteen large bedrooms, a friendly fireplace in the parlor, and a ballroom that served as a public meeting place, and host to all kinds of entertainment.

Mr. Culver built two steamboats for the Wisconsin River trade – the *Lady Catharine* that he piloted between Helena and Portage, and another small boat that he ran between Helena and Prairie du Chien. He also operated the ferry at Helena for a number of years. That ferry ran under several different owners until 1887 when the Wisconsin River was finally bridged.

By the late 1840s, the population was again growing – settlers were attracted to the valley because of the expected development of navigation on the Wisconsin River. Some of the newcomers settled at nearby Wyoming, and it too soon became a bustling community with saw mill, stores, school, lumber yard, and a post office established in 1848.

But river transportation was greatly retarded by low water and rapids, and the Portage canal had not yet materialized, rendering the water route impractical. Hence, a quite profitable business developed in the form of overland transportation. Farmers and teamsters hauled their produce from the Helena area to Dodgeville and Mineral Point, returned with lead for the shot tower, and many engaged in hauling the shot from Helena to Milwaukee, returning with supplies.

The shot tower business had been sold in 1847 to Washburn and Woodman, a Mineral Point law and real estate firm. They operated the tower for about two years, and apparently abandoned the project. Then, in 1853 John Bradford came in from Illinois and took over. About the same time, an entire colony of emigrants had arrived from Prince Edward's Island, considerably increasing the size of the village. Both Helena and the shot tower business boomed.

These were probably the most prosperous years for Helena; the shot business was good, and that brought in a lot of business to the hotels and stores. But the railroad from Milwaukee steadily pushed westward on its path toward Prairie du Chien and the Mississippi River. When it crossed the Wisconsin and passed through Spring Green, as would be the similar history of many small towns, the people of Helena and Wyoming firmly believed that the railroad was the only way of the future, and by 1861, the beginning of the Civil War, operations at the shot tower had been suspended – nearly all its machinery was sold to a party erecting a tower in Chicago. Stores, hotels, and homes were moved, and some simply torn down. The shot tower warehouse was torn down, and its lumber used to construct the town hall at Arena. The stone was used to build a smokehouse.

Helena had been revived once after its near total destruction during the Black Hawk War. But this time, nothing would ever bring it back. From rise to fall, it lasted only 30 years, but what grand years they were!

IRONTON

The state of Wisconsin, in the very early years, held mining interests other than the lead region of the Southwest. In the far north, the Gogebic, Menominee, and Penokee Iron Ranges have produced millions of tons of iron ore. "Red Gold" drew immigrants here to mine the ore needed to satisfy the demands of a growing industrial nation, populating new towns where dense forest and wilderness had once been. Transportation systems like the Milwaukee, Lake Shore, & Western Railway were created to answer the transit needs of the new northern industry.

Although most iron mining in Wisconsin had ceased by the 1960s, the world's industrial revolution benefited significantly from the tremendous contributions of the Wisconsin iron mines, and the industry occupies an important chapter in Wisconsin history. Most noted ranges lie in the far northern part of the state, and extend into the Upper Michigan Peninsula to the east, and into Minnesota to the west. They were discovered by strange variations in magnetic compass readings during geological surveys, and confirmed by visual sightings of the distinctive ore on the surface. Much of the iron ore of these ranges lay close to the earth's surface and forming hills and mountains, making it relatively easy and inexpensive to mine.

Iron ore deposits were discovered and mined

as far south as Sauk County, as evidenced in the stories of Ironton and La Rue. Like many towns that were nurtured to life and prospered around mills or mines, Ironton in western Sauk County rose to become an industrial center in the wilderness because of the spirit and efforts of James Towers, an ironmaster from Crown Point, N.Y. He first came to Mayville in eastern Dodge County in 1850 and began the manufacture of iron products. Thoroughly familiar with the entire iron business as it was developed by that time, Towers was seeking an opportunity for business on a larger scale.

He heard the rumors of unlimited iron deposits in the hills of the Baraboo Valley, so he began exploration of the area, and in the rugged bluffs overlooking a beautiful valley near the site that would become Ironton, Towers found the opportunity he was seeking. His trained eye detected the rich mineral deposits in the rock outcroppings and in the soil, and he imagined a prosperous manufacturing city in the valley below him, bustling with the families of the men who would work for him in his blast furnaces and factories.

After purchasing the property, he returned to

the East to make arrangements for developing his project in the wilderness. He convinced many of his former employees – mostly Irishmen – to move with him to Wisconsin, and to become the vanguard of settlement in the valley of the Little Baraboo River.

The new town suffered its share of hardships while log houses were erected for the families along the river. Then it was a matter of constructing the blast furnace, iron mill and foundry, while preliminary development of the mine was under way. Machinery for the entire operation was shipped to Portage by rail, and then hauled by ox teams and wagons to the new town site, a long, slow, and laborious task.

Four years later, Ironton's furnaces and foundries were hard at work. Charcoal burners were busy night and day converting the hardwood trees into high quality smelting fuel. Ore from the mine on a hillside two miles away was transported to the mill by cumbersome ox carts, where it was smelted and cast into pigs or saleable merchandise items, and then hauled to the nearest markets 20 or 30 miles away.

The superior quality pig iron from the Ironton foundries always found a ready market at

Milwaukee, Chicago, Rockford, and other manufacturing cities for the best prices. Prosperity was at its peak as the output yielded a profitable income.

James Towers did not live to see the greatest success of the business, nor the tragic decline that came as the ore bed began to run out. The property changed ownership several times, and each owner, expanding the scope of the plant, realized a profitable success. But the advance in timber value and a corresponding increase in the cost of producing charcoal, and the plummeting price of pig iron that came in 1890, made the manufacture of iron at a furnace lacking all the modern facilities highly unprofitable.

When James Towers located his mine, he had not discovered an inexhaustible "drift," but rather a deposit of unusual high quality ore of limited quantity. By 1895 the supply was depleted and the company was dissolved. Iron works gave way to agriculture and dairying, and the great gash in the hillside that was once a mine was soon overgrown in brush.

Ironton still remains, although it is no longer the great steel town in the woods.

LA RUE

La Rue didn't emerge as an actual town until 1903, and its short life ended in 1914. Mining of a low-grade iron ore used for paint pigment had begun near there in the 1880s, and the Douglas Iron Mining Company was actively probing for higher grade ore, but with little success.

Then in 1900, W.G. La Rue arrived, bringing with him the diamond drills, and plenty of experience gained in the Minnesota iron ranges. He and his partners incorporated the Sauk County Land & Mining Co. in 1902, and within a short time they had brought up samples of 53 percent iron from several hundred feet below the surface. They leased the land to the Deering-Harvester Co., and by 1903 the mining boom was under way.

This new beginning of successful iron ore production meant business for the railroad, prompting the Chicago & North Western Railway to extend a spur line three and a half miles south to the mine from the main line at North Freedom. Tons of the red rock were loaded into the wooden ore cars and carried away to blast furnaces in Chicago.

The operation seemed to be a sure bet, so by the end of that year, La Rue and his partners incorporated the La Rue Townsite Company. Hotels and a row of company-built cottages soon provided housing for the Norwegian, Swedish, and Finnish miners. Saloons, stores, and a church were established on streets named Iowa, Illinois, Wisconsin, Indiana, and Deering Avenue. A busy little town, La Rue was on the map.

The ore was rich, but as the mines probed deeper, in time another problem became insurmountable. Water filled the mineshafts faster than pumps could take it out. Eventually, the cost was too high to compete with the Minnesota iron ranges, and the operation was simply shut down in 1914.

The miners left to seek work elsewhere, and with no population, businesses closed. Buildings fell into ruin, and La Rue quickly became a ghost town.

When the need arose for an extremely hard quartzite rock in 1917, work trains once again made the rusty rails of the Quartzite spur to La Rue creak and groan. A mile farther south from the remains of the abandoned town lay a vast deposit of quartzite at a place called Rattlesnake Den, and once again the tracks were extended and quarry operations began that continued another 44 years, but the town was never revived. The Harbison-Walker Co., owners of the operation, shipped the material via the Chicago & North Western to plants in Ohio for blast furnace lining and the making of firebrick. But as the steel production process changed, the demand for the quartzite rock diminished, and in 1962 the Baraboo range was again abandoned.

Today, the Mid-Continent Railway Museum, located at North Freedom, Wisconsin maintains the Quartzite spur line and operates vintage steam-powered trains to the mining site as tourist excursions. Adjacent to the authentic 1890s depot that houses railroad memorabilia and gift shop, one can view a host of steam locomotives and cars from the Golden Age of railroading.

JUNEAUTOWN
KILBOURNTOWN
WALKER'S POINT

Solomon Juneau was one of three men who bought in 1835 the first land holdings in the area given the name Milwaukee, a Native

American word meaning "Gathering place by the water." A French Canadian, he had run a fur trading post near the Milwaukee River since 1818. He had attained great wealth through his trading business, and after the United Nation of Chippewa, Ottawa, and Potawatomi signed a treaty in Chicago in 1833 that relinquished a large section of land south and west of the Milwaukee River, Juneau purchased that portion between the river and Lake Michigan. He named it Juneautown, and it quickly began attracting more settlers.

Byron Kilbourn acquired the land on the west side of the river. In heated competition with Juneau, he established Kilbourntown. He made sure that his streets running toward the river did not correspond to the streets on the east side. This accounts for the many angled bridges that still exist in Milwaukee.

George H. Walker built his first log house on the land he claimed just to the south of Juneautown. His town became known as Walker's Point.

By the mid-1840s the population of all three towns had grown, and so had the tension between them. Kilbourn had distributed promotional advertising about the area without any mention of

Juneautown, as if the eastern side of the river was uninhabited and undesirable. But now there had been a bridge constructed connecting the two towns; the Wisconsin Legislature, finding the ferry system on the Milwaukee River inadequate, had ordered its construction. Disputes erupted over the cost of the bridge. Kilbourn and his supporters saw this bridge as a threat to their community. He destroyed part of the bridge in 1845, and over the next several weeks violent fighting broke out between the inhabitants of the two towns. No lives were lost, but several serious injuries were incurred. The incident became known as the Milwaukee Bridge War.

The conflict was finally resolved when the Legislature ordered that both communities share the cost equally. The two towns then began making efforts to mend their differences and reached an agreement in cooperation. The following year (1846) the founding towns were combined; a city charter was ratified and Solomon Juneau was elected the first mayor of the City of Milwaukee.

SINIPEE

I t wouldn't seem likely that a Mississippi River town that had raised to the status of a regular port of call for many steamboats, and that had become a popular shipping and commercial center, could just vanish with hardly a trace. The story of Sinipee, though, reveals the remarkable rise and fall of such a town.

Miners in southwestern Wisconsin Territory found themselves at the mercy of shippers and merchants in Galena, Illinois, the dominant shipping port in the region. No competition meant high prices for supplies and shipment of their only product – lead – that was in high demand in the eastern markets. But the Mineral Point miners thought the businessmen of Galena seemed to be taking a little more than their fair share, so they began searching for an alternate shipping port. They found their answer on the bank of the Mississippi just four miles north of Dubuque where there was an excellent landing, easily accessible for the largest boats. Here they would establish a shipping depot for the lead mining district, and they would call it Port Sinipee. (Sinipee is derived from the Sauk words assini, for "rock" and nipee, for "water." Combined, their meaning becomes "the place of the rock by the water," which accurately describes the towering limestone bluff with its base at the river.)

Twenty-three Mineral Point investors formed the "Louisiana Company" in 1838 and for the sum of $12,000 purchased the riverfront land from Payton Vaughn, who had settled with his new wife in the shadow of the bluffs at the mouth of the Sinipee Creek in 1831, built a log cabin, and operated a cable ferry. Part of the agreement they made with Vaughn obligated him to build a substantially adequate hotel to accommodate travelers at the new village. The company then hired civil engineer, John Plumbe, Jr., to survey the site and act as agent to sell building lots. Plumbe had recently come to the Wisconsin Territory from the east where he had been instrumental in building the first interstate railroad from Petersburg, Virginia to Roanoke Rapids in North Carolina.

Construction began, and by early spring of 1839 about twenty-five commercial buildings had been erected at Sinipee, housing blacksmith shops, warehouses, several stores, a bank, a church, a post office and residences. Payton Vaughn's large hotel, appropriately known as "Stone House," was completed in grand style, constructed with local stone, finished with elegance uncommon to the Wisconsin frontier, fireplaces in every room, and a ballroom occupying most of the second story that served as the social gathering place for the entire community.

It was at Stone House in December 1838, where John Plumbe presented to the Sinipee citizens gathered there his idea to petition Congress to fund the building of a railroad from Lake Michigan to the Mississippi River. He possessed the far-sighted reasoning that a railroad would someday stretch to the California coast, and his road across Wisconsin to Sinipee would be the first link of that transcontinental system. His presentation drew unanimous support, and the proposal was drafted and introduced to Congress by Territorial Delegate G.W. Jones. It received favorable consideration, and the funds were appropriated for the survey. Although it would be many years before the railroad was actually built, it is quite conceivable that the initialization of the United States transcontinental railroad was born at Stone House in Sinipee, Wisconsin.

Large quantities of lead began arriving at Sinipee for shipment down the Mississippi, and a number of St. Louis steamboats made the port a scheduled landing. Real estate values soared as the business traffic increased and more people took watchful interest in the new settlement. It appeared that Sinipee's prosperity was assured, and that it could easily rival Galena, and even Dubuque as a major river port.

Expansion and further development of Sinipee's residential and business areas was planned and in progress when disaster struck the little town of about 200 population in the spring of 1839. The Mississippi swelled with the spring thaw and unusually heavy rains. Most of the village flooded, and although the immediate property damage was not great, the receding floodwaters left behind stagnant pools of slime. Warm summer temperatures followed, and within a short time uncontrollable swarms of malaria-carrying mosquitoes infested the town. At that time, treatment of the disease was unknown, and most of the citizens became ill, and many died. The only hope of survival for those remaining was to vacate the settlement, and after such a short existence, Sinipee was a ghost town.

When the CB&Q Railroad built through the area in the 1880s all the wooden buildings had long ago been dismantled for their valuable lumber or moved on sleds across the Mississippi ice to Dubuque. Its tracks were laid within a few feet of the only remaining structure – the old Stone House hotel. It survived until 1904 when it was consumed by an accidental fire. Eventually, a contractor demolished the remains and used the rock from the walls as fill for a Mississippi dam. In October 1934, Lock and Dam Number 11 was completed, raising the water level behind it. Water now covers most of the land where once stood the incredible little river town, Port Sinipee.

WAUBEEK

The story of Waubeek in Pepin County begins with the story of a man, Cadwallader Colden Washburn. A highly regarded officer for the Union Army during the Civil War, he went on to become the Governor of Wisconsin, 1872—1874. As a successful businessman, the tiny town of Waubeek, which he founded, made him a very wealthy man.

Washburn's ancestors arrived in Massachusetts in the 1630s; both his grandfathers served in the American Military during the Revolutionary War.

Cadwallader Washburn was born on a farm near Livermore, Maine in 1818. He was one of ten children. He and his six brothers achieved much: two became governor of Wisconsin; four were elected to Congress; two served as ministers to foreign countries; one was Secretary of State under Ulysses S. Grant; and three were authors.

With very little money in his possession, Washburn left Maine at the age of 21, intending to settle somewhere in the Mississippi River Valley. Over the next few years, he worked as store clerk and school teacher, and managed to study law. At age 24 he was admitted to the Wisconsin Bar and set up a law practice in Mineral Point. As the California Gold Rush drew the interests of Southwestern Wisconsin's lead miners away, lead production diminished drastically. But yet another fortune lay in the vast pine forests that covered Northern Wisconsin. In partnership with Cyrus Woodman, the two speculators began buying large tracts of the northern pine forest, including 12,000 acres on the Chippewa River just a few miles north of present day city of Durand. The land surrounded a well-known Chippewa River landmark—Waubeek Mound—a hill that was named for an Indian princess. (The name was eventually adopted as the township name as well.)

Washburn built a lumber mill at the foot of Waubeek Mound in 1855 utilizing an eighty horsepower steam engine. Capable of cutting 60,000 feet of lumber per day, this was the largest pre-Civil War mill in Wisconsin.

As the War Between the States began heating up, Washburn organized and led the 2nd Cavalry Regiment of the Wisconsin Volunteers. A distinguished unit for their campaigns in Texas and Tennessee, Washburn's regiment served admirably in the Union Army. Washburn retired from the military at the close of the war with a rank of Major General.

When he returned to Wisconsin after the war, he discovered that his lumber mill had been poorly managed in his absence, and he was facing insurmountable debts. His best option was to sell the business to Knap, Stout & Co., another large lumber mill concern of Menomonie. Washburn relinquished to the buyers his timber land holdings as well, but not for immediate cash payment. Instead, he agreed to future delivery of a certain amount of lumber from the mill. When he finally collected a few years later, the lumber had quadrupled in value; Waubeek had made Cadwallader Washburn a very wealthy man. He went on to become a two term US Congressman and a one term governor of Wisconsin.

Waubeek continued to prosper. Many dwellings and businesses were established with the Knap, Stout & Co. mill employing 100 men at its hub. A fine hotel operated by John McAuley, saloon, blacksmith shop, dance hall, a large general store with an abundant assortment of goods, and a Baptist church surrounded a public square with beautiful trees. A school was built in the community in 1861, its first teacher, fifteen-year-old Alice Drake. The land of the vicinity was rich and fertile, capable of producing good crops of corn, wheat and potatoes.

This beautiful little village was situated on the North Pepin and Chippewa Falls stage road near the lower end of Nine Mile Island, a large mass of land where the Chippewa River splits into two channels. The second channel, then referred to as "Nine Mile Slough" was the better rout to float logs, and had been chosen as the location for the Chippewa Boom chartered by the Wisconsin

Legislature of 1853. It was the only place between Chippewa Falls and the river's mouth where a boom could be constructed to safely collect and sort logs, and assemble log rafts. The rafts were then maneuvered downstream to the markets along the Mississippi River.

Waubeek was not only a place of beauty, but also of economic advantage, in the midst of abundant pine forest, and on the banks of a navigable river.

Prosperity ended for Waubeek as fire broke out and destroyed the mill in 1870, never to be rebuilt. With its productivity gone, the village died as well. Even though it had become the home of the largest sawmill in Wisconsin at the time, the community apparently was no able to diversify economically. People left; buildings were moved or abandoned; in a short time, Waubeek was nothing more than a memory.

The land is now privately owned, used for hunting and recreation. But Waubeek Mound still rises above the Chippewa River as a reminder that a thriving village once was there.

PORT ULAO

Befpre coal, steamships on the Great Lakes burned wood as the primary fuel—a lot of it! Fortunately, in those days wood was in ample supply, as much of Wisconsin was covered by forest. For that same reason, agriculture had not yet advanced beyond small plots scarcely adequate to maintain the needs of a family and a few head of livestock. Clearing the landscape of timber to make way for cropland became a prime goal, and in some areas the shipping interests benefitted. One such area was twenty miles north of Milwaukee.

James T. Gifford recognized the potential of a highly profitable business venture in Ozaukee County on the banks of Lake Michigan. He arrived in 1847 from Illinois where he had served in the state legislature, and immediately purchased a large tract of land adjacent to the lake. His timing was perfect; farmers were beginning to settle in Wisconsin, and steam powered vessels were gaining a foothold in Great Lakes shipping.

A large portion of Gifford's land lay on a table-flat plateau overlooking a steep bluff near the lake shore. Two structures were the essentials of

Gifford's plan: first, a wooden pier was built extending a thousand feet into the lake from the shore; then a wooden chute was constructed from the high plateau down the steep bluff to the pier.

As the settlers cleared their land of trees, they hauled the wood by teams and wagons to Gifford's wood yard, grateful for the payment Gifford offered. It was cut to proper length, and sent down the long, steep chute. From there it could be easily loaded onto the steamships docked at the pier. Gifford's wood business was an instant success.

Harbor development had not yet begun on the Wisconsin shores of Lake Michigan. Even though Milwaukee's population had grown, its port was up the Milwaukee River, the mouth of which was obstructed by a sandbar that made navigation to the port difficult. Captains of ships headed to Chicago and in need of fuel favored easier docking at Gifford's pier.

The village of Ulao was surveyed and platted on fifty acres by Luther Guiteau; it attracted many inhabitants and became a busy, important Great Lakes shipping port. Gifford built a sawmill and warehouse at the lakefront, and his great ambitions acquired a charter from the Wisconsin Legislature to construct a plank or macadam paved road from Ulao to the Wisconsin River. Only three miles of the road was completed, but it was the first macadam pavement used in the state, made from charcoal produced from the local forest mixed with burned clay. The surfacing process was quite successful, as was the cork wood operation to supply steamships. However, for unknown reasons, Gifford sold his interest to Great Lakes Captain John Randolf Howe after only three years.

Not long after the close of the Civil War, the wood supply depleted, and coal was rapidly becoming the choice fuel. Activity at Port Ulao diminished; residents moved away, leaving only the area farmers. The once bustling village was quiet, and the beach was empty.

Today, the only remaining original building is "Ghost Town Tavern" near the intersection of Interstate Hwy 43 and STH 60, where Ulao Road begins and continues to the lake. This was the route of James Gifford's first macadam road.

RICHLAND CITY

When Isaac Wallace and Garwood Green located their claim on the high delta at the confluence of the Pine and Wisconsin Rivers in 1848, they may have been aware that this choice piece of real estate had been occupied before by an ancient people. They might have deduced that by observing the many burial mounds in the surrounding area. The more recent Native Americans may have left traces of their occupation, as well. But Wallace and Green weren't concerning themselves with what had been, but instead they were looking forward to what was to be. They foresaw a grand city on the banks of the Wisconsin River, and their foresight proved to be accurate.

Modern day archaeological studies of this particular region have unearthed thousands of artifacts that clearly indicate the continuous human habitation of the area for the past six thousand years or more. The exact origin of the ancient cultures is not known for sure, or if the more recent American Indians are their direct descendants. Nonetheless, the new pioneer village that was about to rise up on the delta on the east side of the Pine River was not the first human habitation there.

To the newly-arrived pioneers it seemed like the perfect location for a city: the level plateau lay 30-40 feet above the surface of the river, providing ample safety from flooding; good fertile soil meant plentiful crops as a food source; forested hills were abundant with wild game; two rivers provided means of transportation in three directions.

And so the village was platted in 1849. Perhaps this was just a good stopping off point for other pioneers on their way to find their place in this new land, but certainly some of them decided this was their utopia. Richland City grew at such an alarming rate, that in its third year, a new partner to Wallace and Green, A.C. Daley, platted a large addition to the village. A couple of years later, an additional 64 blocks platted by Jacob Coffinberry doubled the size of the town.

Owners of numerous stores and service businesses such as blacksmiths, carpenters, tailors, shoemakers, jewelers, and doctors had recognized Richland City as an advantageous location to set up shop. A post office was established, and the town was fast becoming one of the most important river ports on the Wisconsin between Prairie du Chien and Portage. Nearly all the goods shipped to all of Richland County arrived by Wisconsin River steamboats at Richland City, and this new port with its hotels, saloons, and even a distillery—well-known for its fine wines and liquors—had been designated as one of the favorite overnight stops by lumber raftsmen on their journeys to the Mississippi River markets.

The territory's largest flourmill and a sawmill—both steam powered—were erected at Richland City; both were vital elements in the town's economic success. Schools and churches were established; Richland City was destined to a great existence.

As the Milwaukee & Mississippi Railroad etched its way across Wisconsin with a planned destination at Prairie du Chien via the Wisconsin River Valley, the people of Richland City were overly confident that such an important milestone in the development of the state would surely pass through their important spot on the map. They had even named one of the streets "Railroad Avenue." But now, destiny was about to dispense a dose of bad medicine.

Edward Brodhead, the chief engineer responsible for railroad construction, had, in 1852 scouted the route down the Wisconsin River Valley. Following a course along the northern shore, the line would pass through several existing villages, but on that side of the river, the bluffs hugged the river bank, making construction difficult on such little space. Although a south side route involved more bridging, traversing the Wisconsin near Lone Rock and routing across the flat prairie through Avoca, Muscoda, and Boscobel seemed more practical. It seems odd that the people of Richland City didn't know that this route had been finalized in 1853.

The railroad triggered a series of events that spelled disaster to the village on the delta: because they could no longer compete with the regularity of trains, the Wisconsin River steamboat traffic declined drastically, reducing the commercial shipping activities at Richland City to almost nothing. Now, all incoming goods arrived by rail and were received at the Lone Rock depot.

Although there had always been a ferry service across the Wisconsin at Richland City, the people there had unsuccessfully petitioned several times for a bridge. But because a bridge was built ten miles downstream at Muscoda in 1868, and because Muscoda also had the railroad, it became the important agricultural shipping point in the region, diverting even more business away from Richland City.

Twenty years after the Milwaukee & Mississippi Railroad bypassed the river town, another sprig of hope came when the Pine River Valley & Stevens Point Railroad Company built a narrow-gauge line connecting Lone Rock and Richland Center, the county seat and flourishing city. But alas, a railroad of any kind through Richland City was not to be. By then, the village on the delta was facing yet another compromising condition: the Wisconsin River's main channel was shifting as it had done in other places and times. Its unrelenting current was eating away the sandy bank that was Richland City's waterfront. Already, two streets parallel to the river and numerous building lots had vanished as the earth collapsed into the water. Residents and businesses alike had moved away from the emanating catastrophe, relocating in the new neighboring village of Gotham, far enough from the river to be out of harm's way, upriver to Lone Rock, or downriver to various other communities. Richland City's post office was removed and re-named to Gotham, where the narrow-gauge railroad passed the new depot.

Reason for the changing river channel has never been determined for certain; some claim that wing dams built upstream from Richland City altered the currents; some say the closure dam on the opposite shore placed there to enhance the ferryboat operation was to blame; and yet, some think it was just the will of nature.

Whatever the cause, all attempts to combat the situation proved futile. Because riverboat traffic on the Wisconsin had all but ceased, the government discontinued all procedures of channel improvement, and Richland City continued to disappear. By 1885, its population had dropped from 1,000 to just 75 people. What had once been the site of a robust, prosperous metropolis now lay at the bottom of the Wisconsin River.

Today, not much remains of Richland City; the Wisconsin River now occupies nearly the entire original plat of the village on the delta.

PAUL SEIFERT—
RICHLAND CITY FOLK ARTIST

For several decades around the turn of the twentieth century, a German immigrant named

Paul Seifert traveled through rural Southwest Wisconsin, stopping at different homesteads and chatting with the owners. He complimented each farmer on his property and before long convinced him that his place was picture-perfect and should be immortalized in a painting. Seifert, of course, would be just the man for the job. For about three dollars, he promised a beautiful watercolor on 21" x 28" paper. Seifert's sales pitch must have been convincing, and his paintings became so popular that eventually over a hundred of his rural scenes were displayed in farm houses all over Richland, Sauk, Grant, Iowa, and Crawford counties. In one case, Seifert even painted six versions of the same farm. Today Paul Seifert's paintings are highly appreciated as examples of rural Midwestern folk art.

Paul Seifert arrived in Wisconsin in 1867, and for the rest of his life he remained closely connected with the land and the people of the state's Driftless Region. Born in 1846 in Dresden, Saxony, he grew up surrounded by teachers and students at the Free Mason Institute in Dresden, a preparatory boarding school for boys where his father was the head schoolmaster. Paul Seifert later attended a trade school (the exact school and trade are unknown), and—just prior to his emigration—also the Royal Academy for Agriculture and Forestry in Tharand, Saxony, for one semester. A photo labeled "winter semester 1866/67" shows Paul Seifert in his student uniform at the Academy.

These were turbulent times in Europe and especially in the Kingdom of Saxony. In 1866, decisive battles in the Austro-Prussian War were fought on Saxon territory, with Saxon troops fighting on the losing Austrian side. In 1867, as a result, Saxony lost some of its previous independence and became a member of the newly founded North German Federation, the precursor of the German Empire, which was dominated by Prussia.

It is not known if the political and military situation influenced Paul Seifert to emigrate, but on September 14, 1867 he boarded the ship *Eugenie* in Hamburg and two days later sailed for America. The *Eugenie* arrived in New York on November 2, and Paul quickly moved on to Richland City in Richland County, Wisconsin. In 1867, Richland City was a boomtown at the confluence of the Wisconsin River and the Pine River, a major stopping point for riverboats between Prairie Du Chien and Portage. Today the city no longer exists, having been abandoned because of a river that continually changed its course.

Paul Seifert quickly adapted to his new surroundings. He befriended a German family, the Krafts, who had come to Richland City from Baden via New York, and in 1868, Seifert married their daughter, Elizabeth. Together the young couple bought land nearby, started a vegetable garden, and sold their produce in neighboring communities. A year later, the first of their four daughters was born.

With many mouths to feed, Seifert made a living for himself and his family in various ways. He opened a taxidermy studio, and—while Elizabeth and his daughters tended the vegetable farm—traveled the Wisconsin countryside with a sketch pad, paper, pencils, and paint. Sometimes he created a painting on the spot, while at other times he made a sketch and finished the work at home. His most productive decade was the 1880s. His earliest known farmscape was painted in 1879; his last may have been painted in the late 1910s, as it includes a 1915 Ford Model T. Seifert depicted rural life as a simple but detailed tableau. That could include colorful barns and houses; farmers' children playing in the field; someone shooting a fox nearby; lazy cows grazing in the meadow behind a barn—a beautiful and idyllic world, without the hardship that farming in the late-nineteenth century also entailed.

In the late 1940s, Paul Seifert's watercolors were discovered by Jean Lipman, a prominent folk-art scholar and long-time editor of *Art in America* magazine. She not only wrote about them in her many publication, but also started collecting Seifert paintings herself. Before long the watercolor farmscapes from Wisconsin became sought-after collectors' items across the nation.

While Paul Seifert is remembered today mostly for his paintings of farms, he was also keenly interested in the history, the landscape, and the people of Southwest Wisconsin. In particular, he was fascinated by Native Americans. On his many excursions throughout the region, he found and collected Native American artifacts. Many of these, such as projectiles and scrapers, he donated to the Wisconsin Historical Society and regional museums.

Maybe that is why his name is connected with one of the "cave mysteries" in the region. After

Seifert's death in 1921, stories appeared in Wisconsin papers, citing an article that purportedly had been printed years earlier in Vienna, Austria. As the tale goes, Paul Seifert had stumbled upon a hidden cave in the Wisconsin River bluffs filled with skeletons and Native American artifacts. He had sent some of the objects to an archeologist friend in Vienna, who supposedly travelled all the way to Wisconsin, inspected the cave for himself, and was stunned by the treasure he saw. After that visit, however, Seifert destroyed the entrance to the cave to hide it and its contents forever. His friend returned to Europe, and Seifert never shared the location with anybody else. This story was often told in connection with other stories of Indians who had "vanished" in the bluffs. Fact or fiction, people are still looking to find the "Indian mystery cave" in the bluffs of Richland County.

TAYCHEEDAH: VILLAGE BY THE LAKE

The first Europeans to explore the Lake Winnebago area found an Indian village on the southeast shore. The chief of this colony was Sar-ro-chau; he and his Winnebago band would be long remembered by all the early traders and settlers because of their friendly manner and their willingness to help the newcomers when other Indian tribes became hostile. The old chief took part in the War of 1812, and he died soon after. His son, Charatchou, aided the American militia in the pursuit of Black Hawk's warriors in 1832.

During the years of exploration and settlement of the Wisconsin Territory, the overland travel route from the Green Bay region to Fond du Lac and the prairies beyond followed the eastern shore of the expansive lake. Travelers passed through the old Indian camping grounds, and the pioneers became intrigued with the possibilities of this being the perfect location for a settlement. A mile of level land covered with groves of trees stretched back from the sandy shore of the lake to a picturesque, 200-feet-high ledge, with another extensive area of level, wooded land. The view of the lake from this higher level was incredibly beautiful, and the entire area seemed ideal for a village or city.

A settlement was started at Taycheedah in 1839. The first permanent settler to build a home there was Francis D. McCarty, who was soon followed by more settlers from the east. He built and managed a hotel, later to be owned and operated by Nathaniel Perry until the old structure became inadequate to accommodate the many travelers who came to or passed through the village. Perry then built a much larger hotel, and under his management, this hostelry was known from Green Bay to Chicago for its genuine hospitality and the excellence of its meals.

B.F. and J.T. Moore opened the first general store in Taycheedah in 1841, serving the entire region northward to Brothertown. By 1850, a large flour mill and a sawmill operated in Taycheedah; the thriving village had also attracted a tin shop, dry goods stores, and two blacksmith shops.

Governor James Doty assisted in the construction of the first public schoolhouse of the county at Taycheedah in 1842, and the first school bell heard there was a gift from Col. Henry Conklin. He acquired the bell from the dismantled steamer *Advocate* that was wrecked on the Hudson River. Edgar Conklin was the teacher in this pioneer public school that served the population of both Taycheedah and Fond du Lac.

The beauty of the location seemed more

attractive than the earlier established Fond du Lac, and for a decade more than half of the prominent men of Fond du Lac County lived in Taycheedah. It became the social and cultural center of Fond du Lac County, and its commercial importance shadowed the neighboring settlement of Fond du Lac.

The shortcoming of Taycheedah was its harbor, never a good landing place for anything but smaller vessels. However, the first steamboat to navigate on Lake Winnebago waters, the *Manchester*, Capt. Stephen Hoteling, master, made its maiden voyage to Taycheedah, and the town became the southern terminal with Neenah the northern, and Oshkosh and Fond du Lac intermediate stopping ports.

Situated at the southernmost end of the lake, Fond du Lac's harbor was superior to that of Taycheedah, but there seemed little else to attract growth in the early times. The land was low and marshy, and to the early settlers there, the drainage problem must have been nearly insurmountable. Every spring when the snow melted from the surrounding hills, flooding occurred, creating a great disadvantage. However, the strategic location made Fond du Lac the more logical site for a city. In addition to the excellent harbor conditions, it was anticipated that the major railroad lines would likely converge there; that important factor apparently far outweighed the problems with the terrain.

Although Taycheedah was the larger community, the rivalry for supremacy continued through the 1840s. About 1848, however, Fond du Lac began to attract settlers in such numbers as to establish its domination for all time. This result was due largely to the prudence of Dr. Mason C. Darling. He had acquired enormous amounts of real estate at Fond du Lac, and donated a site for the courthouse as well as lots for many new businesses. At a time when money was scarce in this struggling new territory, businessmen were eager to take advantage of such offers of free land. Speculators in Taycheedah were still holding their building sites at premium prices, and therefore lost the edge.

The decline of Taycheedah started before the Civil War. Nearly all the old families that had been there in the beginning and had built Taycheedah to a thriving community were gone, moved to Fond du Lac and other cities, taking with them the businesses that had made the village prosper. But the village never completely vanished; as late as the 1920s, there was still a good public school, a Methodist Church, a general store, and a post office served a population of one hundred fifty people. Passengers could board trains that stopped on signal at a little weather-beaten shed, although there was no station agent or freight service. Today, homes and resorts garnish the lake shore for miles, and Taycheedah is as beautiful as it ever was.

ROCK ISLAND

At the mention of the name, *Rock Island*, thoughts come to mind of that picturesque city along the Mississippi River in Illinois. But there is a place in Wisconsin by that name, as well; a 912 acre island lies just one-half mile from the northern shore of Washington Island, which is about four miles off the tip of the Door County Peninsula. This tiny speck of land isolated by the cold waters of Lake Michigan is now an uninhabited Wisconsin State Park accessible only by boat. However, it once was the site of a lively little fishing village populated by no less than 100 people for several decades of the Nineteenth

Century.

Long before the fishermen settled there, though, Rock Island had been home to a tribe of Potawatomi Indians. Archeological studies show that human habitation was present as early as 600 B.C., and documentation indicates the presence of French explorers, army, and fur trappers in the 1600s.

The Indian tribe from Ontario was, perhaps, the first to settle and establish a fortified village on Rock Island in the mid-1600s. They remained there until well into the 1800s, and remarkably co-existed with various other groups, including the colony of fishermen who established their cozy little village in a cove on the island's southeast shore.

By the early 1800s the fur trade was on a decline in Wisconsin, but because the population there was beginning to grow, the number of ships carrying passengers and supply cargoes on the Great Lakes with destinations of Green Bay increased. Entering the bay, however, formed by the peninsula (now known as Door County) was treacherous for sailing ships; adverse winds could slam a vessel and its unsuspecting crew into the sixty-foot-high cliffs at the north shore of Rock

Island guarding the bay entrance. Owners and captains of some thirty ships petitioned the US Government in 1832 for the construction of a lighthouse there, and four years later, a government crew came to the island, quarried stone from the bluffs, and built a forty-foot light tower and a keeper's house. It was the first lighthouse in Wisconsin, and the first on Lake Michigan. (There is still a light in operation adjacent to the original location.) The first keeper of the lighthouse was David E. Corbin, a veteran of the War of 1812, former member of the Fort Howard garrison, and one time employee of the American Fur Company. Because the lighthouse was located at the edge of a steep cliff that extended in both directions, Corbin had to cut a road through heavy forest nearly a mile long to a landing on the south shore. All of Corbin's supplies, including drinking water, had to be carried along this road to the lighthouse.

Even though it was a great distance from the little fishing village, the lighthouse and its keeper were always considered part of the community. Corbin remained at his post until his death in 1852.

When the lighthouse was finished and put into operation in 1836, the population of the fishing village grew with people who, until then, had used the island only as summer quarters. The community had the good fortune of having young John Boon among those earliest permanent settlers. His knowledge of the Chippewa language served to help maintain a peaceful co-existence with the large number of Chippewa Indians sharing the island.

Most of the villagers were fishermen; fishing was the basis for the island's economy, as buyers from eastern markets were paying fine prices for fish by the barrel. The industry created other work, as well. More than a dozen coopers kept busy producing barrels, and loggers made their livings cutting cordwood, selling the fuel to the captains of steamships.

Life on the island was good, but it had its share of hardships, too. Islanders had no escape from adverse weather conditions; at times, the isolation made existence difficult. By the late 1850s, other parts of Door County were developing and populating, including Rock Island's closest neighbor, Washington Island. Gradually, some of Rock Island's residents opted for the better conditions elsewhere that more than compensated for the superior profits gained from island fishing.

But the village still remained, occupied by a number of hardy souls. There must have been a great deal of optimism among them, as in 1863 a log schoolhouse was erected, although at the time there were only seven families with school-aged children. Three years later, the leader of the community, John Boon died, and within a few more years, the population dwindled. After the last local fisherman left Rock Island in 1890, the only permanent resident was the lighthouse keeper. Occasionally, visitors came to hunt, fish, or cut logs, but no one wished to stay there permanently.

Then, in 1910, Chester Thordarson bought 800 acres of Rock Island (all but the lighthouse reservation). He and his wife lived in one of the abandoned village homes that he had rebuilt, and constructed a stone water tower nearby. But the accommodations proved to be only temporary; he soon engaged in the construction of several stone buildings of Icelandic design on the more suitable southwest shore of the island, the most impressive of which is the magnificent boathouse and great hall, said to be reminiscent of the Icelandic parliament building.

Thordarson was born in Iceland in 1867; he came to America at the age of five with his parents.

Self-educated by his hunger for knowledge beginning at an early age, he eventually resided in Chicago where he continued his education in public schools and was employed in the field of his greatest interest—electricity—by the Chicago Edison Company. He later left that employment to start his own business, and went on to produce high-voltage transformers, and became quite wealthy.

But his greatest passion became Rock Island. It reminded him of his native land—Iceland—and it served as the perfect setting for Thordarson to live in and study nature and pursue his love of botany. Among the many structures of his little Icelandic village was a greenhouse built on a fieldstone foundation. In addition to the great hall that took twenty masons three years to build (at a cost of a quarter-million dollars) were cottages and a lodge where he and his wife frequently entertained guests such as Clarence Darrow and Prohibition-era Chicago Mayor "Big Bill" Thompson.

Thordarson died in 1945 and was buried in the same island cemetery with John Boon, the leader of the original fishing settlement. His estate was willed to the family, however, in 1964 it was sold to the Wisconsin Conservation Commission for use as a state park.

Today, Rock Island reveals only traces of what was once a thriving fishing village. A replacement lighthouse structure built in 1858 remains in its restored condition as a museum on the northern bluff overlooking Lake Michigan, and is a highlight attraction for park visitors.

Visitors are welcomed at the south shore landing by the magnificent stone boathouse and great hall, also serving as an exhibit hall for the island's wildlife and artifact displays, and celebrates the life of its creator, Chester Thordarson.

A passenger ferry from Washington Island will take you to the landing on the south shore, but from there, it is up to you to stroll the beaches, explore the trails through the forest to the lighthouse, experience nature, and to discover what life may have been like on Rock Island in yesteryear.

WEST BLUE MOUNDS
(POKERVILLE)

West Blue Mounds was its original name, and to it belongs the distinction of being the earliest permanent settlement of Dane County. With a population of 500 at its peak, this little village had the atmosphere and romance of a typical mining town, the excitement of a pioneer outpost, and the uproar of a community where land values have suddenly "boomed."

Long before the boom, long before any white man set foot on this land, the Native American Indians considered the large hill—Blue Mounds — a sacred place. They named it for the bluish haze that surrounds its two peaks, believed to be the smoke from the pipe of Manitou, the Great Spirit dwelling at the summit. The area around Blue Mounds was rich in surface lead ore; the Indians gathered it and used it as a trading commodity with the French trappers/traders along the Wisconsin River as early as the 1700s.

When prospector Ebenezer Brigham came there in 1828, this region was still part of the Michigan Territory. From Massachusetts he had roamed the west for several years until he learned of the potential wealth in lead mining around Blue Mounds. There, he discovered a rich vein of lead ore, staked his claim of some 1400 acres, and built a substantial log cabin, making him the first permanent resident of what is now Dane County. The cabin was strategically located a mile from the mine, adjacent to the first overland route blazed through the Wisconsin wilderness connecting Fort Howard (Green Bay) and Fort Crawford (Prairie du Chien). Because the lead mine attracted more prospectors and settlers to the area, "Brigham's Place" soon became a store, hotel, and tavern and was a popular stopping point on the only trail across Wisconsin. (A few years later, 1835, Regular Army soldiers cleared a 30-foot-wide path through heavily wooded areas and marked the trail across open prairies with wooden stakes or mounds of rocks. The Military Road passed Blue Mounds and "Brigham's Place.")

Within a short time after Brigham's arrival, a small settlement began to grow with houses, stores, hotels, a doctor, a blacksmith, a harness maker, and even a wagon builder; the village was then christened "West Blue Mounds."

As the Black Hawk War erupted in the spring of

1832, West Blue Mounds was seriously threatened, located directly in the path of Chief Black Hawk and his tribe of Sacs who had raided several other settlements, massacred, and took hostages. A rudimentary fort was hastily constructed on a small hilltop near the village to accommodate all the families, miners, farmers, and residents of the immediate area where they stayed for two weeks. Brigham and his people feared for their lives. Although Black Hawk's warriors were pressed northward by the pursuing militia, and no attacks on the fort occurred, two scouts from the garrison, out to determine if the hostile tribe was near, were ambushed and mercilessly killed within plain view of their companions at the fort. About two weeks earlier, a citizen was killed by Indians while he was getting water from a well.

After the Indian War ended, the territory was opened up for further settlement, and life at West Blue Mounds resumed its move forward. The first school in Dane County was built there, and a post office was established, Brigham as postmaster.

The Barnum Circus even came to the village! Since there were still no railroads at the time, the elephants were walked out from Madison carrying packs of circus equipment on their backs. One of the notable features of the exhibition was the sensational race between ostrich and horse, a popular amusement of the day.

Valuable lead mines afforded the small village prosperity, and the influx of adventurous new-comers rapidly drove up the population. Fortunes were made overnight, as well as tragedies and loss.

Common in all mining towns, the night life held its dark secrets. Gambling became rampant; the village became known far and wide as "Pokerville." Fortunes were won and lost every night at the tavern tables, not only by the miners, but by visitors as well. Liquor flowed freely in the town's taverns, general stores, barrooms, and a ten-pin alley; brawls and bloodshed were common, and killings were not unheard of.

Rough as it was, Pokerville owed its remarkable financial success largely to lead mining. The product was hauled to Galena, Green Bay, or Chicago, and rendered attractive profits to the people of Pokerville, continuing through the years of the Civil War. All during this time, Ebenezer Brigham, the founder, remained one of the most influential citizens of his community. He was instrumental in getting West Blue Mounds established as a town, and acted as its representative in the first meeting of the Territorial Legislature in 1836. He died at Madison in 1862.

After the Civil War, demands for lead sharply decreased, and Pokerville's economic "boom" declined. Many miners left the area, but a few families remained, turning to farming, keeping the village alive.

Although Pokerville had long been a regular stagecoach stop on the improved Military Road, in 1874 a government contract for a mail route from Madison to Dodgeville was awarded to a new stage line headquartered in Pokerville. Timan Knutson, a Norwegian emigrant who had served with the 23rd Wisconsin Infantry during the Civil War, drove the mail and passenger stagecoach. To fulfill the contract, he made two round-trips per week between Madison and Dodgeville, each taking three days to complete.

The final stroke that in time delivered Pokerville to ghost town status was the building of the Chicago & Northwestern Railroad in 1881. It missed the village by merely a mile to the east; a depot was constructed, and the present-day village of Blue Mounds was born. The inhabitants of Pokerville were soon gone, taking with them their homes and businesses to the new Blue Mounds, Mount Horeb, or Cross Plains.

Nothing of Pokerville remains today. Straddling Hwy 18 at the Dane/Iowa County line just west of Blue Mounds, the site where once stood general stores, hotels, saloons, shops, and a ten-pin alley—the village known as Pokerville—is now only a picturesque memory in the shadows of the highest hill in Southern Wisconsin, Blue Mounds State Park. If you visit the locale, careful observation may reveal some of the original structures moved to the village of Blue Mounds from Pokerville so long ago.

PARIS

Throughout the Nineteenth Century, Southwestern Wisconsin remained quite active in lead mining. During that time, countless small settlements sprang into existence as prospectors poured into the region by the thousands. There always seemed to be a spirited entrepreneur ready and willing to set up shop, speculating on substantial profits by supplying the miners with essential needs—everything from picks and shovels to flour, to... yes, whiskey. Many of these settlements prospered and grew, surviving even the demise of the mining industry, and remain today as thriving, healthy villages and cities. Some managed to retain only a handful of residents through the years, and exist as merely a warm and fuzzy, lonely little residential community.

Some endure in name only, perhaps distinguished by a significant landmark, or some lesser relic vestige, or in numerous cases, nothing at all. Representing this category, two Grant County ghost towns share similar events in their short-lived existence, making their histories colorful and unique.

French (or possibly French-Canadian) born adventurer, Martial Detantabaratz arrived in the region in 1828. It is likely that he spent the first few years there prospecting, perhaps with little success, or, perhaps he lacked the enthusiasm to continue with the strenuous labor-intense mining operations. He did possess, however, the ambition to become the founder of a settlement. He had chosen land on the west bank of the Platte River near the confluence of its two branches, about three miles from the Mississippi River. He laid out his town in 1835, called it Paris, probably because of his French heritage, and built a store and a lead smelting furnace. A few years later he added a tavern, and in 1839 he constructed a toll bridge across the Platte River, the first known structure of its kind in Grant County.

Paris continued to attract more settlers; the town grew. But by then, Martial Detantabaratz was experiencing financial difficulties with one of his creditors, David Bates of Galena, Illinois. In the Nineteenth Century it was still acceptable practice to challenge an adversary to a duel with deadly weapons; Detantabaratz chose swords, as he had once been a dragoon in the French Army. Bates had no experience with such a form of combat, wanted no part of it, and wisely withdrew. Nothing is known about the resulting agreement between the two men; however, Martial Detantabaratz's problems apparently did not end there, as in 1842 he hanged himself and his young town also soon perished. It is not known where his body was buried.

Other than the same name that was adopted for the township, nothing remains of the original Paris in Grant County, Wisconsin.

FAIR PLAY

Another early Grant County settlement, originally named Hard Town, was the result of a substantial lead ore discovery by John Roddan in 1841. He had arrived three years earlier, built a cabin, and then took up prospecting until he located the rich vein of ore.

News of Roddan's strike spread, and he soon had hundreds of neighbors who swarmed in from Galena, ten miles to the south, and from Hardscrabble (now Hazel Green), six miles to the east. But with the impetuous waves of prospectors, all seeking quick fortunes, trouble was bound to erupt. One of the common issues in any mining community was accusations of claim-jumping. These dilemmas, usually between two sole individuals, often came to deadlock, occasionally resulting in bloodshed. Such an incident escalated to that status in Hard Town; two miners were about to publicly engage in battle, and a crowd had gathered to witness. Perhaps it was noticed that there existed an unequal advantage among the combatants; it is uncertain who in the crowd called out: "Let's have fair play here, and render unto Caesar the things that are Caesar's!"

In response, the gathered crowd began chanting: "Fair play, fair play..."

That must have caused the two opponents to reach a peaceable resolution; the duel was avoided, and the town got its new name, Fair Play.

A post office was established, a number of stores appeared, and a combination church and school was built. The town was incorporated in 1845 with over 500 residents. Optimism soared; many believed that Fair Play would advance to a major city. But instead, the village retained the characteristics of a rough-and-tumble pioneer mining camp. One of its taverns, "The Lighthouse," became regionally well-known for its high stakes games and "knock-down, drag-out" fights. It seemed that Fair Play wasn't quite ready for a more sophisticated culture.

Another claim-jumping duel threatened in 1846. Once again, the dispute was successfully reconciled, and the duel did not take place. This incident, however, was noted as the last known threatened duel in Grant County.

The late 1840s saw a drastic reduction in the area's lead production. Ore prices dropped, and miners were lured away to the California gold rush. As quickly as it had grown, Fair Play's population dwindled. New mineral discoveries in 1856 were thought to be the way of the town's revival, but unfortunately, it did not long endure, and another rapid decline followed.

Recognized as the oldest remaining town hall in Wisconsin, the limestone structure is the only original building left. Until recently, it was still in use as a township meeting hall, but has since been tastefully incorporated into a private residence, still visible, to remind us of the fascinating little village of Fair Play.

DOVER

E dward Brodhead, construction engineer for the Milwaukee & Mississippi Railroad, owned land at the site that is now the village of Mazomanie. He bought the land in 1853 while surveying the route the railroad would take from Madison to the Mississippi, following the Wisconsin River Valley. Speculation of using the waterpower of a Wisconsin River tributary located there loomed in his head, as the road grade would provide containment for a substantial mill pond.

His scheme materialized, perhaps sooner than he anticipated.

The growing village of Dover, two miles to the west, had been well-established since 1844. Its beginning was unique, as the original plans for the new settlement were actually laid in Liverpool, England in 1842. The British Temperance Emigration Society and Savings Fund, organized by three men—Robert Gorst, Charles Wilson, and Charles Reeves—was a co-op of sorts, that was to buy government land in the Wisconsin Territory, and make that land available to the society's interested investors. They gained the trust of many with the agreement that each settler would receive eighty acres of farmland, with a 14 X 20 log house already constructed when they arrived, plus a portion of the land cultivated with crops already growing.

Charles Wilson, acting as the Society's agent and two companions traveled to Wisconsin the following year when enough money had been raised. They found the ideal place along the Wisconsin River about twenty miles west of the new Territorial Capitol, Madison; plenty of open land with fertile soil, uninhabited for miles, except for Potawatomi and Winnebago fishing and hunting parties wandering about.

Wilson went to the land office in Mineral Point and purchased a large amount of the wild land for $1.25 per acre. When he returned, he surveyed the 80-acre farm plots, and with his companions and other hired men, they began preparing fields and building cabins.

The first eleven families arrived from England in 1844, with many more on the way; the village had its start. For the next two years it was called Gorstville, in honor of one of its founders. The new arrivals found vast, unobstructed prairies, ideal for agriculture, good water, beautiful surroundings accented by the wooded hills and stone-faced bluffs lining the river. The biggest problem facing these settlers was that they were not good farmers; many had little or no knowledge of agriculture. With little money and few provisions, many fell ill and died that winter.

By 1847 the Society had acquired 9,600 acres and the population had increased despite all the adversities. However, the leaders of the community—Gorst, Wilson, and Reeves—were experiencing great difficulty in relations with the tenants; their duty was to collect rents, purchase land, erect housing, make improvements, and pay taxes. But there was little money available among the dissatisfied occupants; financial troubles became insurmountable, and the Society's function was dissolved.

The name had been changed to Dover, and even during these hard times, the village continued to grow to over 250 people. A post office was established in 1850, and within a few more years there were several stores, a blacksmith shop, cooperage, hotel, and a school. Ferry service provided transportation across the Wisconsin River.

Then came Edward Brodhead and the Milwaukee & Mississippi Railroad on its important march toward Prairie du Chien. Brodhead, by then, had taken over the presidency of the financially embarrassed rail company. He personally visited Dover to negotiate the purchase of land for a depot and siding tracks. The location he chose was owned by a Mr. Culver who set an unreasonably high price for the land. Brodhead made a counter offer at a reduced amount, but Culver wouldn't budge.

Perhaps Culver's refusal to lower the land price was Brodhead's excuse to remove the plans for a depot at Dover, and instead, place it at his property two miles east, where a few cabins now occupied a small settlement he called Mazomanie, named in remembrance of an Indian Chief. His scheme to establish water power there, and to develop a settlement village had become reality.

Dover's population had flourished to over 700, but with no railroad depot, it seemed doomed; many houses and some businesses were relocated to Mazomanie to be nearer the railroad. After the Civil War, a young soldier, John Appleby, who had grown up in Dover, returned home, and nearly revived the town. Until the war had interrupted his work, Appleby had invented a device that would eventually revolutionize farm machinery. He developed the idea for the twine knotter from watching his mother knit.

The first demonstration of his grain binder was held in a wheat field just across the road from his house. (That field is adjacent to the roadside park and the Dover historical marker, and is still used as cropland today.) A large crowd gathered to witness the performance, however, it ended in disappointment. The device did not work properly and broke down several times.

With the confidence, encouragement, and investment by Dr. E.D. Bishop, Appleby continued to develop the machine, and by the mid-1870s he had it perfected. William Deering, a major farm machinery manufacturer, witnessed another successful demonstration. He made a deal with Appleby to produce the invention, and within a short time, the twine knotter was a common component on all binding machinery.

But sadly, by that time, nearby Mazomanie had absorbed most of Dover's population. All that remained were the farms and the hotel. No one was left to share John Appleby's joy of accomplishment.

Today, the remains of Dover are few: on the north side of US Hwy 14, in a roadside park is a Historical Society plaque marking the center of the lost village, a small cemetery (where, ironically is buried Mr. Culver who stubbornly priced his land too high for a depot and caused Dover's demise), and the adjacent field where John Appleby demonstrated his knotting device; and on the south side of the highway stands the old hotel, now a private residence.

BRIDGEPORT

F ive miles up the Wisconsin River from its confluence with the Mississippi are the sparse remains of old Bridgeport. The village was near the river level in a narrow ravine on the north bank, which is the only break in the bluffs for many miles. There was little room to build; its Main Street was hardly wider than an alley.

It was at this point on the Wisconsin River where an important crossing was established in the early 1800s, and still remains as the crossing point for US Hwy 18 and State Hwy 35. More history clings to the Bridgeport crossing than any other in the state. When the Military Road —the first major road built across Wisconsin—was put through from Green Bay to Prairie du Chien, initially intended for use by US Army troops and to haul supplies to Fort Crawford, a pole ferry was established at the Bridgeport crossing. But the road soon became the main thoroughfare for fur traders carrying their wealth of pelts to be shipped off to European markets.

Then came the great tide of immigration into western Wisconsin and northern Iowa. A steady parade of ox- and horse-drawn prairie schooners carrying families and their belongings flowed over the road.

As surveyed by James Doty and US Army Lieutenant Alexander Center in 1832, most of the road followed along heavily traveled Indian trails. By 1835, Army troops from Fort Crawfor under the command of Col. Zachary Taylor (12th US President) had cleared a 30-foot-wide path from Prairie du Chien to Poynette, 110 miles through the wilderness. (Soldiers stationed at Fort Howard worked from that direction until the two units met mid-way.)

Hercules Dousman, American Fur Company agent, originally owned the land on which the village of Bridgeport was started. He sold the ferry to Peter Barrette who had the contract for carrying mail between Prairie du Chien and Platteville. Barrette converted it to a cable ferry, using the river's current to propel the craft. He operated the ferry service nearly twenty years and did a bonanza business.

Another small hamlet at the opposite ferry landing was called Brooklyn, later renamed Banfill after a local and prominent land owner. By 1838 it had a post office, a saloon, a few stores, and in later years a sawmill and a hotel. But because of its swampy location, mosquito infestation, and frequent flooding, the village never amounted to much.

Bridgeport, however, continued to prosper. Two events helped advance its development: (1) the Milwaukee & Mississippi Railroad completed the line through Bridgeport and beyond to Prairie du Chien; and (2) a toll bridge crossing the Wisconsin River replaced the ferry.

Soon the village grew with hotels, blacksmiths, saloons, general store, grain elevators, warehouses, and a stockyard. By the 1870s, Bridgeport had boomed into becoming the major shipping point of agricultural and lumber products for a large region. Long lines of wagons piled with wheat and produce, cattle on the hoof, and wagonloads of cut limestone (some of which was used to build the new capital at Madison) waited their turn to cross the bridge.

John Lawler, construction engineer and railroad agent at Prairie du Chien, took over ownership of the bridge after a fire had destroyed part of the town and caused some damage to the bridge. He began repairs and improvements, including a floating drawbridge span, using a similar design as his pontoon bridge he built for the railroad's Mississippi crossing at Prairie du Chien.

Serious damage was done to the bridge once again in 1892 by an ice storm. It was then that a shingled roof was built over it, and it continued to carry traffic across the Wisconsin River, even into the new age of motorcars and trucks.

This new age of traffic, however, rendered the old wooden toll bridge inadequate and out-dated. The state purchased the privately owned bridge in 1929, and two years later, its steel and concrete replacement was finished and in operation, this time toll-free to the traveling public. The old relic was the last toll bridge on the Wisconsin River.

Just as the first bridge had boosted Bridgeport's prosperity, the new high span caused the village to decline, as it rerouted traffic to the bluff, bypassing the river town.

Then, in the fall of 1936, a raging fire destroyed nearly the entire town. The blaze had practically wiped Bridgeport out of existence. Some residents, at first, desired to rebuild. But the overall enthusiasm lacked, and original Bridgeport eventually became another Wisconsin ghost town.

OIL CITY

Although the first settler in the area that would become Monroe County arrived in 1842, provenance of the village near his homestead wouldn't come for another twenty-eight years. And, although Oil City, in 1870 received its name from a fraudulent act, the dastardly deed itself probably had little to do with the birth of the hamlet.

Esau Johnson, the first white man to establish a permanent home there along the Kickapoo River, just a few miles north of present-day Ontario, came in much the same manner as so many other pioneers arrived in the wilderness. He and his family had come down the Wisconsin River on a log raft to the mouth of the Kickapoo, where they stayed and worked on Mr. Haney's farm until that fall. After exploring the Kickapoo River Valley on foot, Johnson chose a spot that he liked, and then returned to Haney's in a hollowed-out log boat. There he hired two helpers, and on October 1, 1842 arrived back at his homestead with his family and household belongings. Within five days, Esau and his hired men had cut logs and constructed a house that his family moved into.

By the time Wisconsin Territory became a State in 1848 and Sheldon Township was designated within Monroe County, Esau Johnson's family had added another son, and Esau was operating his lumber mill. The splendid Kickapoo River Valley had started to attract more settlers, and during the next decade, the settlement grew not only in population, but a business community spawned as well, with general store, cooper shop, grist mill, several sawmills, and a tannery. Money was appropriated to build the township's first school near the settlement, but the number of school-aged children among the population apparently out-grew the size of the school, and soon another was erected amidst the embryo village. (Another replacement came in later years at the same location; school was in session there until 1959.) The school also doubled as a church; Sunday School classes were conducted regularly by a Baptist minister from the neighboring village of Ontario.

At the first Sheldon Township meeting in June 1858 in Graham's Grist Mill, officers were elected, and from that time forward, all meeting and elections were held at various business places. Several attempts to gain permission to build a town hall in later years failed. Not until 1911 was one constructed, which is still in use today.

It was 1865 when smooth-talking Mr. Tichnor arrived. He claimed to be an expert oil man, and evidently no one displayed any reason to doubt his word. In a short while, he had the people of this un-named community convinced that the land where they lived was perfectly suited to produce oil, and he was prepared to prove it. Within a few days he announced the news: he had indeed struck oil!

People of the township accompanied him to his oil discovery site along the upper Kickapoo to see it for themselves; after touching and tasting, everyone concurred that the black substance seeping out of the ground was in fact oil.

Tichnor wasted no time initiating the Gem Petroleum Company, negotiated high-priced land leases from the area property owners, and began offering shares of stock in the company. Everyone naturally wanted in on the pending oil boom, and the stocks, already in big demand, sold quickly. As a "favor" to his constituents, he sold most of his controlling shares as well.

The citizens of Sheldon Township were excited; they were about to become rich beyond their imagination. Work commenced promptly; several wells descended into the earth, but the only substance they yielded was water. Not ready to give up, the well diggers sunk the well at the site of Tichnor's original discovery to a depth of 700 feet, certain that success was imminent. A gusher shot twenty feet in the air—of clear, pure artesian water.

It was soon discovered that Tichnor had secretly buried a barrel in the ground and tapped it for the crude oil it contained. But by that time, the oil tycoon—the head of Gem Petroleum was gone without a trace, and with him, all the money he had swindled from the citizens of Sheldon Township. Although Gem Petroleum ceased to exist, the wooden structure with the overflowing tank of artesian water would remain as a sort of monument, to remind the people of their fleeting prosperity. They affectionately called it "the derrick."

Yet, even without the prospects of great oil wealth, there were promising signs of growth and development. Millen Graham laid out the Village of Oil City—the commonly accepted name—in eight blocks, seventy-two lots, with a sixty-foot-wide Main Street through the center. (That Main Street is now part of State Hwy 131.) The plat was recorded at the County Clerk's office in Sparta on June 11, 1870. Within a few years, every lot was occupied by homes and businesses. Oil City's post office was officially established in time for Christmas, 1873.

Then, during the last decade of the Nineteenth Century, another event gave Oil City great hope for prosperity. The Kickapoo Valley & Northern Railway Company planned to build a rail line from Wauzeka on the Wisconsin River up the Kickapoo River Valley to Wilton. A depot would be located at Oil City. The citizens of Sheldon Township signed a petition granting railroad aid.

The rail company, however, fell twenty miles short of its projected destination of Wilton; the line was built no farther than La Farge. Once again, Oil City lay victim of a failed promise, and many of its residents lost a lot of money.

After the turn of the century, more attention and patronage was given to nearby towns of Norwalk and Wilton. Oil City's progress diminished; it could not compete with the larger commercial communities that were situated on the

Chicago & Northwestern Railroad. In time, Oil City businesses closed, and some were destroyed by fires; the post office was discontinued; its population began moving out and the abandoned homes were torn down, the land becoming additional cropland for adjacent farms. The last remnant—the school—closed in 1959, and another chapter in Wisconsin history ended. Oil City remained in name only.

OLD BELMONT

Right from the very beginning, the village of Belmont—designated as the seat of government for the newly formed Wisconsin Territory—was doomed as the permanent capitol city for the future state. Located in the highest populated area of the territory (which included all of present-day Wisconsin, Iowa, Minnesota, and part of the Dakotas) it seemed the logical place, amidst the lead mining region in Lafayette County. But it was not to be. Although there is today a Village of Belmont in Lafayette County, it is not the same exact location as the original "First Capitol" Old Belmont.

The name was derived from French explorers'

name given to the nearby "mound," a landmark hill, its peak visible for twenty-five miles in any direction. They called it "Belle Monte" or beautiful mountain. The first settlers started to arrive in 1827.

The US Congress created the new Wisconsin Territory in 1836. President Andrew Jackson appointed Henry Dodge, a prominent citizen of Mineral Point, then the largest city in the territory, as governor. Dodge's appointment probably stemmed from his heroic involvement in the Black Hawk War four years earlier. For it was Henry Dodge who was instrumental in retaining the loyalty of the friendly Wisconsin Winnebago tribes, and preventing them from joining forces with the hostile Black Hawk. Had that happened, the outcome of that conflict might have been quite different with the annihilation of all white settlements in the lead mining region. Dodge had also initiated the hasty construction of several log forts throughout the region, thus providing additional safety for the settlers. Al-though only a few skirmishes occurred in the Wisconsin mining region resulting in but a few casualties, Henry Dodge remained a hero in the eyes of the mining communities.

Dodge recognized the importance of placing the capitol where it would be most advantageous. Since the most concentrated population of the entire territory was the lead mining region, it seemed the best location. Land speculator and promoter, John Atchison of Galena, Illinois, assured Dodge he could build the capitol city, including the four proposed buildings to accommodate the legislature functions: a council house for the legislative sessions, a Supreme Court building, a governor's residence, and a lodging house for the legislators.

Governor Dodge was satisfied with Atchison's plan, and with his choice of land located near "Belle Monte," ten miles southwest of Mineral Point, however, it soon became quite controversial among the leaders of other communities wishing to be considered. Despite Atchison's issue of an affidavit stating that Governor Dodge had no interest in the city of Belmont, the matter still caused a great deal of unrest. It was thought that Dodge and Atchison, in consort, had acted in their own speculative interests, hopeful that Belmont would become the permanent capitol city.

Needless to say, when the legislature convened October 25, 1836, the matter of capitol location became a major debate, only after the Governor in his opening address, admirably stated that he would not stand in objection to any other location chosen by the representatives of the people.

Newspapers of various towns throughout the territory heavily criticized the choice of location, adding more fuel to the debate. Belmont, by that time, had a newspaper, the *Gazette*. Its editor loyally defended the establishment of the capitol with reassurance that the accommodations there were quite adequate.

That, however, was an overstatement. The thirty-six legislators found their lodgings rather uncomfortable. The lodging house had not been completely finished as promised, with no means of heat and entirely lacking in furnishings. They were required to sleep on the floor, covered with only their own coats to protect them from the cold. It is no wonder why that first session lasted only 46 days!

The Council House, though, was finished and adequately furnished with wooden tables and chairs for the legislative meetings, although only one wood stove to provide heat to the two-story structure. Because there was no lumber yet readily available in the territory, finished oak lumber to construct the 25 X 42-foot building had been purchased in Pittsburgh and transported by steamboat on the Ohio and Mississippi Rivers to Galena, Illinois, and then hauled the twenty-five miles overland by wagon to Belmont. The interior was finished with lath and plaster, making a very substantial structure.

It was soon evident that Belmont would not remain the permanent capitol of the future state, Wisconsin. Ex-federal Judge James Doty—who had already been influential in Wisconsin's development—was now a shrewd speculator who realized the capitol location issue would lead to a troublesome obstacle. But he had the solution: shortly before the legislature session began, he had acquired land at Four Lakes (now Madison) and had platted a city on the isthmus between the two large lakes, Mendota and Monona.

As the capitol location debate was introduced and continued for many days, Doty arrived at Belmont and informed the government body of his proposal to locate the new capitol at Four Lakes. At first, it was viewed with condescension, but Doty, possessing a rather persuasive character, sweetened the deal among the representatives. When the session adjourned December 9, 1836, not only had this first legislature entered 42 laws in the books—statutes that would shape the new State of Wisconsin twelve years later—but it had also placed the new seat of government in the new capitol city of Madison, and thirty-six members of this governing body left Belmont as proud owners of various real estate properties there.

The first 46-day session of the 1836 Wisconsin Territorial Legislature was the last to be held in Belmont. And even though its glamorous future had raced away, and many of the businesses promptly moved on, Belmont remained a village for quite some time, maintaining its post office and several businesses until 1867. Chief Justice Charles Dunn, who had come to his post in 1836, bought the lodging building and converted it to a fine dwelling, where he and his family lived for many years until his death. Although the annual sessions of the Supreme Court were held in Madison, much of Dunn's official duties were carried out from his Belmont residence. It was in that house that his lovely daughter, Catherine, was married to Wisconsin's first Governor, Nelson Dewey in 1848.

But in time, the village lost its residents and the one remaining store; the major contributing factor—the railroad. The route for the Chicago, Milwaukee & St. Paul missed the village by three miles to the south. Villagers moved the distance to be near the new rail station. The Belmont name and the post office went with them. Charles Mappes erected the St. Charles Hotel, and Belmont had its second coming. What was left of the prior village came to be known as Grandview.

A few years later—1884—the Chicago & Northwestern Railroad established a station just north of Grandview. This little community was named Leslie, consisting of a town hall, a school house, a store, a deserted creamery, a few houses—one of these being the old Dunn house—and the railway station.

By that time, both of the only remaining capital structures—the Dunn house and the Council House—had been moved a short distance and were, for some time, used as cattle and hay barns.

In 1910 the Wisconsin Federation of Women's Clubs began raising funds to save and revive these important pieces of Wisconsin history. The buildings were inspected, and although they were in a sad state of repair, they were deemed sound and restorable. The Council House was moved back to its original site in 1924 and restoration began. The lodging house was returned to the site in 1956 and was restored. During this time, the project was under supervision by the Department of Natural Resources.

Today, the site is in the care of the Wisconsin Historical Society, open to the public, and is part of the beautiful Belmont Mounds State Park. When you visit, you may even hear the debating voices of 1836 echo through the halls.

SPRINGVILLE

A branch of the Bad Axe River flows silently along the floor of a deep, narrow valley a few miles north of Viroqua. And above it on a sloping hillside the abandoned old red brick Springville School stands sentry over a few scattered houses. At the hill's summit lie in their final rest the remains of those once residents of this lively little village in the bucolic valley. It's all that is left of Springville.

John Graham and his three sons, Thomas, Baker, and Lamech, came here in 1846. The valley with its swift-running stream was appealing; it was the perfect spot for a mill.

The Grahams built a substantial log cabin, and later that year, William McMichael—John's son-in-law—arrived with his family to settle there as well.

The following year, 1847, tragedy struck; Thomas Graham fell ill and died. He was the first to be laid to rest in what would eventually become the hilltop cemetery.

Construction of the three-story mill was underway on the riverbank. Its two-run of stone, turned by an undershot wheel, powered by the stream's swift current was operational in 1848.

As more settlers were attracted to the rich farmland of the area, Graham laid out the village; a post office, Emil Strang its first postmaster, was established in 1849, and within a short time, the streets of Springville—named for the abundance of fresh-water springs in the valley—were lined with various stores, a carpenter shop, and a doctor. The first schoolhouse was built just north of the village in 1850. (It was replaced with the red brick school in 1892.)

John Graham and his sons continued to operate the gristmill for seven years, when they built a larger three-run of stone mill about 100 yards downstream. The old mill was torn down.

About the same time, E.C. Officer opened a shop making furniture. Philip Buffleur built the Springville Hotel. The busy little village of

Springville rivaled nearby Viroqua that was then just beginning its early growth.

John Graham died in 1862. As the founder of the village, he had lived a full life; he had built two successful mills; he had buried two wives and married a third; and he had raised eleven offspring.

At the close of the Civil War, a lumber mill was added to the list of businesses in the village, and Springville continued to flourish. Six years after John Graham's death, the Graham Mill was sold when son Lamech Graham formed a partnership with Alfred Glassborn and created Eureka Mills with a 40 X 40 stone structure at a cost of $9,000. Soon after, the old mill was destroyed by fire.

Eureka Mills continued to operate until it, too, was heavily damaged by fire in 1881. But it was rebuilt and repowered with steam.

Situated in a narrow valley, Springville was continuously vulnerable to devastating floods. The last mill there was completely washed away in 1907. The little village by then had lost many businesses and the population was drawn to the larger nearby towns. Westby and Viroqua had the railroad.

July 1951 delivered the final catastrophic blow

with another flood, this time drowning a family of six.

Today, County Highway B threads its way through the valley past the few remaining reminders that a thriving town once was there.

NEWPORT

S peculation may have been taken to a higher level when the village of Newport boomed. However, deception and a series of unlawful acts during the years of its short existence brought it crashing down just as quickly.

About two miles downriver from present-day Wisconsin Dells, three small settlements, all independent from the others and occupying land on both sides of the Wisconsin River, eventually joined together to establish one village that would be called Newport. The name was optimistically chosen, as this was the farthest point on the Wisconsin that steamboats could navigate from the Mississippi during periods of high water.

Sometime in the late 1840s a ferry service linked the east and west banks, and Newport began to grow. Built on the site of a previously abandoned Indian village, Newport was situated along a popular western migration route, and it was becoming a favorite stopping place for the crews of lumber rafts after negotiating the treacherous dells—a stretch of the river contained between shear rock walls not more than fifty feet apart— coming down from the northern pineries.

In 1850 Newport's growth was boosted with the news of a charter granted by the Legislature to the founders, Joseph Bailey and Jonathan Bowman, to construct a bridge across the river at their settlement. A couple of years later, the formation of the Milwaukee & La Crosse Railroad, with plans to set its course northwesterly across the state, created great speculation for Newport. Bailey and Bowman promptly approached the rail company's president, Byron Kilbourn, in an attempt to convince him that Newport was at the most favorable spot on the Wisconsin River for a crossing. Kilbourn was in agreement.

To further escalate Newport's rapture, another charter was obtained for building a dam across the river. Harnessing the water power for mills and factories would assure Newport of great success and prosperity. When this news reached the people, in no time the real boom was at full throttle. Merchants, hotels, and other businesses moved in, and within a few years, the population had ballooned to more than twelve hundred.

The Milwaukee & La Crosse Railroad was finally awarded the land grants to finance construction of the line. But Bailey and Bowman had no assurance that Kilbourn still intended to have his railroad cross the river at Newport. To better the chances, they transferred 200 acres of Newport land to Kilbourn, and as additional incentive, they also signed over their State Charter authorizing construction of the dam.

Within a few months, Kilbourn had persuaded the State Legislature to pass an act authorizing the incorporation of the Wisconsin River Hydraulic Company, which also allowed his dam construction at several locations other than Newport. At the same time, he was buying large tracts of land about two miles upriver. To keep this all secret, Kilbourn even had his surveyors work during hours of darkness by lantern light.

But his plan didn't stay under wraps for long. Rumors suddenly became facts. When the residents learned of the new town that had been platted just up the river, and the railroad bridge would cross the Wisconsin there, near pandemonium broke out. Newport, with all its development done in good faith, was doomed, and there was no hope for changing the course of the railroad. Kilbourn held the distinct advantage. He controlled the railroad, and he now had the blessing from the State Legislature to build a dam at a point of his choosing. And both would be located at his town that he so arrogantly called Kilbourn City.

This was a crushing blow to the residents and businessmen of Newport. Their only hope of survival was to comply with the coming trend. If the railroad was coning to Kilbourn, so would they.

By the time the Milwaukee & La Crosse Railroad pushed its way across the Wisconsin in 1857, a large portion of Newport had been abandoned. There wasn't even a charter for a dam there anymore—no water power or anything else to keep businesses and factories there. Within a few years, Newport had died a painful death. Only a very few residents remained.

As for Kilbourn and his city, justice prevailed. In a later investigation conducted by the Legislature, Byron Kilbourn, president of the railway and mayor of Milwaukee, was found to have used $900,000 of railroad money to bribe members of the Assembly, Senate, a Supreme Court Judge, and even the governor and his private secretary. By these means, he had won the competition between several railroad companies to receive the land grants, and had manipulated the authorization for a dam and bridge away from Newport. He was eventually convicted of his fraudulent acts, and the scandal ruined Governor Coles Bashford, who had actually cashed in for $15,000.

Kilbourn City became Wisconsin Dells in 1931, it was said, to promote tourism... or, perhaps, to shun the shame of its founder.

Newport became a memory.

ORANGE MILL

For all practical purposes, the little village of Orange Mill, located just two miles southeast of present-day Camp Douglas in Juneau County, had all the right things going for it. The main road leading to Chippewa, Eau Claire, and Minnesota passed through it bringing a constant flow of emigrants and others bound for the great West; the Little Lemonweir River furnished a most splendid water power for mills; and it had the Milwaukee & La Crosse Railroad and a depot. If for no other reasons, these elements should have propelled Orange into becoming a prominent city.

It is unclear just when the first settler came to Orange Mill. Prior to 1837, (the year of the treaty with the Winnebago in which they ceded all of their land east of the Mississippi River) the only white people in the Lemonweir Valley were a few French-Canadian fur traders. Juneau County was formed by the State Legislature in 1859 when it was split from Adams County with the Wisconsin River as the dividing boundary, however, the first permanent settler in the county was recorded as arriving in 1838.

In a report filed with the *Mauston Star* newspaper in June 1859, the Village of Orange Mill was already well-established. Mr. Spence of La Crosse (58 miles west by rail) had erected a dam and grist mill on the Little Lemonweir River, and Marcus Weed operated a first-class rotary sawmill, producing lath and finished lumber. These two mills provided the essentials for the rapidly growing population of the area.

Soon a small settlement grew up around the mills and took on the same name as the township that had been designated in 1857. Jonathan McKinstry served as the first postmaster beginning in 1859 at his mercantile, where he and his son kept busy dispensing dry goods, groceries, and all other commodities common to a country general store. The first school in Orange Township was built at Orange Mill.

The well-kept Orange Hotel, owned and operated by Marcus Weed, was a credit to the community with the finest accommodations; travelers could expect "a good table, a clean house, and a good bed."

Then came the railroad. Building its way across Wisconsin, the Milwaukee & La Crosse placed a depot at Orange Mill with Mr. Loomis as the Station Agent. (Just two miles northwest, another village—Camp Douglas—grew from a logging camp, providing wood fuel for the locomotives.) New overland roads were surveyed and prepared for travel into Monroe County, and to Necedah and Grand Rapids (now Wisconsin Rapids) and into the northern pineries, bringing those places miles closer to the railroad. Orange was becoming the hub of a large trade area, and it was anticipated that this little village was destined to become one of the most flourishing cities in Juneau County. Great potential lay waiting for the capitalist, merchant, and mechanic seeking a place where the judicious outlay of a little time and effort could realize rich rewards.

But even after the turn of the Twentieth Century when Camp Williams was a major military training facility, Orange Mill remained the sleepy little village it had always been. The railway depot had been destroyed by fire in 1869 and was replaced by only a small shack that remained in service until 1922. A cluster of small motel cabins were built along the highway, sometimes used to house overflow troops from Camp Williams, but that seemed to be merely a temporary boost.

So, what happened to Orange Mill? Just as it is unclear when the village began, is also unclear when it ceased being a village. The Great Depression, perhaps, had a profound impact with the failing economy. Today, nothing remains of a metropolis; dairy farms now occupy the land. However, some remarkable old edifices are still present, even though they are in   decaying condition. A visitor to the site may still view the shabby old school, its rusted bell still in the tower above the entrance; and across the road stands the majestic old Orange Mill on the bank of the Little Lemonweir, some of its tumbled-down machinery still visible through glassless windows. Beyond the mill, the rubble of motel cabins lay in the woods. And the rest is just a memory.

THE CLARENCE BRIDGE

On the east bank of the Sugar River about three miles southwest of present-day Brodhead, once was the bustling little village of Clarence. Settled in 1841, it was first known as Tenneyville; brothers A.D. Tenney and B.J. Tenney platted the land, sold lots, and established a small store. The settlement soon had a hotel, blacksmith shop, a steam-powered furniture factory, and the first physician in the area. The post office was established in the Tenney home, and a school district was organized. By 1856, Clarence was a flourishing village, anticipated to become a major metropolis of southwestern Wisconsin. That, of course, did not happen, as the railroad chose the location of Brodhead for its depot, and as with so many bypassed small villages of that time, Clarence sadly withered away.

At first, as there was no bridge spanning the Sugar River, Jacob Ten Eyck, the resident nearest the river, kept a raft on which he ferried the people of the community and travelers. A bridge was finally built, but every year it washed out with the spring floods. Then in early fall of 1864, heavy pilings were driven at each bank, and construction began on a unique span bridge, 130 feet in length with a sixteen feet wide driveway. It was the only one of its kind, built by a Racine, Wisconsin contractor named Hulburt. It was raised on the ice during an exceptionally good season for such a project. But an early spring and high water forced the contractor to rush the finish, cutting away the underpinning before he was completely ready; however, no serious effects resulted.

At that time, covered bridges were not uncommon; within a few years, the Clarence Bridge was enclosed and roofed, but it was never painted. Watchful township supervisors discovered that the tremendously heavy superstructure was slowly settling; the eight inch crown had fallen to five inches. Although the contractor had been paid in full and the work accepted, he returned to reinforce the main framework by spiking in on each side heavy arches made with two thicknesses of two-by-twelve planks, requiring thousands of board-feet of lumber.

The reinforcement arches seemed to be adequate for quite some time, however, it was later evident that the structure was still settling, and another attempt was made to strengthen the bridge with iron suspending rods. It was left this way for several years, but the crown entirely disappeared, leaving a flat floor. About 1907 it was decided to do what should have been done in the beginning. A concrete abutment was built under the bridge in the middle of the river. The end abutments were also reconstructed with concrete, and this made a very stable bridge. Until that time, the Clarence Bridge had been one of the longest single span structures of its kind in Southern Wisconsin.

In its day, the bridge played some sinister roles. Before the turn of the twentieth century, holdups were frequent in the shelter of the bridge; highwaymen would often hide themselves in the timbers of the bridge's roof, and when a likely looking team would drive into the bridge, the thugs would drop from hiding and gather their loot with very desirable privacy. Horse thefts were also common, the robbers using the same techniques as their brothers in crime who sought cash and other valuables.

In later years, the bridge, once again, was part of a criminal act when the police of two states were searching for Fred Hartin, confessed murderer. Hartin had committed the dastardly deed in a little cabin across the Rock River and then came to Beloit, but managed to evade police and fled before he was arrested.

In his flight he reached the covered bridge just ahead of a group of officers. Seeing them approaching, he slipped under the bridge and hid on one of the big beams over the water. The fugitive lay in this lair for the entire night while the officers paced back and forth in the covered span overhead, guarding against Hartin's attempt to use the bridge as a means of escaping to the west. When they finally went to a nearby farmhouse at dawn to use the telephone, Hartin realized his opportunity, and he fled.

A year and a half later, Hartin was captured in the east by operatives of the Diamond Detective Agency. During his confession, he told of how the covered bridge at Clarence had helped him to escape.

The Clarence covered bridge served travelers of southern Wisconsin until 1931. As motorcar and truck traffic increased, the structure was deemed inadequate; regrettably, the old landmark was destroyed when a new bridge was erected to meet the needs of the time.

TURTLEVILLE

Abraham Lincoln, under the command of Capt. Jacob Early, camped along Turtle Creek in 1832 while scouting for Chief Black Hawk. This was the area where the township of Turtle would eventually be organized, and where the village of Turtleville would sprout. Its name comes from the tribe of Winnebago known as *Turtle*.

About four years after the tumultuous Black Hawk War, Wisconsin was declared a Territory, and within another year, a treaty with the Winnebago (who during the Black Hawk War were friendly allies of the US Militia) opened up the vast wilderness to settlement. Growth progressed rapidly in the southern regions of Wisconsin, offering emigrants plenty of opportunities to begin their new lives. Many came from Pennsylvania, Massachusetts, Vermont, and New York. Although brothers John and Abel Lewis of Pennsylvania weren't the first to settle in Turtle Township, they were the first to settle in 1838 on the spot along Turtle Creek that was soon to become the Village of Turtleville. When they arrived, they found a small band of Indians camped on the south side of the stream, but there is no indication that there were ever any conflicts. They chose that particular location for the good water power potential of Turtle Creek, and constructed a log house there, even before they received title to the land. The following year they built a sawmill, and soon after, they opened the first store in the entire township. Louis Ellenwood added his blacksmith shop, and the village began to expand. A Baptist Church was built; the first regular services were held in 1840 when a minister from Beloit came each Sunday. He was paid one dollar for his service. The church was an important part of community life; farmers came more than five miles from the prairies to attend the Sunday morning services.

The stone schoolhouse was erected that doubled as a meeting place for the earliest business of the township, the first meeting recorded in 1846.

By 1850, the Village of Turtleville, at a busy crossroads eight miles east from present-day downtown Beloit, was one of the prominent communities in the area.

At that time, a wealthy Englishman, William

Hodson arrived in Turtleville. His installation of a sizeable flouring mill and a distillery gave Turtleville its biggest economic boost; his large operations employed many village residents. In time, though, Hodson would be a main factor in the hamlet's demise.

Overlooking his distillery, Hodson built an imposing mansion on the bank of Turtle Creek, Greek revival in style, seventeen rooms with twelve-foot-high ceilings, multiple fireplaces, and a wide plaza garden facing the stream, beautifully landscaped and planted artistically with snowballs, lilacs, peonies, and lilies, giving the premises the appearance of an elegant English country estate. In the cellar were arched vaults that stored the "spirits" produced in the distillery. (This house remained until 1979.)

Another tiny settlement less than two miles east of Turtleville that had been established in 1840 with a tavern serving as a stagecoach stop was the location of the Chicago & Northwestern depot, first known as Shopiere Station (later changed to Tiffany) and in 1857 a post office was established there.

Even though Turtleville had been missed by the railroad, the village continued to flourish with

Hodson's distillery keeping the economy alive... until the Civil War broke out in 1861.

This proved the beginning of Turtleville's darker pages of history. William Hodson, owner of the distillery, happened to be a Southern sympathizer, as many Englishmen were. When the war started, he refused to affix the US Government tax stamps on his whiskey, as was mandatory; he shipped barrels of liquor concealed under wagonloads of potatoes.

Unbeknownst to Hodson, one of his employees was a government agent. Needless to say, Hodson was arrested and the operation was shut down. All his property including the distillery, flour mill, and his mansion was confiscated. When Hodson failed to pay some $98,000 in taxes and fines, the property was sold to the highest bidder for only $3,000 on the Janesville Court House steps in 1876.

After the Civil War, Turtleville became a deserted village. The "boys" that had gone off to fight no longer had any interest in farming or the small community life when they returned. With Hodson and his businesses gone, with the mills and blacksmith shop gone, and with a large portion of the population gone, so was Turtleville's prosperity.

After a time, the church building that had played such a vital role in the social well-being of the village was purchased by the Orfordville congregation, was dismantled and moved to that community. The rest of Turtleville gradually faded away.

Today, all that remains of the original settlement is the cemetery and the historic Turtleville Iron Bridge that was built on Lathers Road across Turtle Creek in 1887 by Milwaukee Bridge and Iron Company. It is still in use.

As for the Township of Turtle, much of its land has been gobbled up by encroaching Beloit, an airport, and two interstate highways. The hum of traffic noise has replaced the quiet solitude of a rural village.

THE PINERIES— WISCONSIN LUMBER

When the American frontier began to push westward beyond the Appalachian Mountains, to the prairies of northern Indiana and Illinois, and then to the vast plains across the Mississippi, the pioneers were faced with a problem they had never experienced before—lack of building materials. Where they came from in the east, there had always been an abundant wood supply. But on the treeless plains of the west, they were forced to turn to alternate construction methods. Absence of timber meant fewer difficulties in creating clear farm land, but how and with what to build homes, barns and fences became a challenge. One solution was to make use of the sod that covered the prairies; this plentiful material sufficed for a time, but to satisfy the desire for structures of a more permanent nature, something better was needed. The only option was to transport good building materials from the nearest source.

The abundant forests of the Great Lakes region provided the best answer. Woodland extending westward from the New England states covered northern Michigan, Wisconsin and Minnesota with a seemingly inexhaustible supply of desirable pine timber, a wealth that far surpassed any world treasure.

The heavily-forested lands of Wisconsin were primarily the northern two-thirds of the state, comprised of a thirty to fifty-mile-wide band of hardwoods at the southern edge, then mixed hardwoods and conifers, and surrounding the headwaters of the St. Croix, Chippewa, Black, Wisconsin, Menominee and Wolf Rivers, pine was the predominant species.

White pine lumber was the preferred building material, as it was light-weight and easily workable. But equally important, its buoyancy made it ideal to transport by floating on the waterways, whereas the dense, heavier hardwoods tended to sink to the bottom of the rivers.

Northern Wisconsin held the ideal conditions

for pine timber, and the lumber industry; the glaciers that once covered most of the region not only pulverized rocky terrain to a sandy soil perfect for the pine forest growth, but they carved out the many riverbeds that provided the all-important means of transporting the logs to the sawmills. Long before any railroads were built into the forest regions, the rivers were most useful to the lumber industry. During the spring, as a result of the melting heavy snowfalls all winter, the high, fast-moving currents of the rivers provided a powerful energy to send the millions of logs downstream to be distributed to the many mills for processing into useable lumber. They flowed to th Great Lakes, and mostly to the Mississippi River, the waterway that was most instrumental in the building of the American West. Wisconsin lumber was even freighted to the eastern markets, as well, until commercial lumbering began in the Virginias.

Even though the virgin pine forests were there, and the rivers were there, logging and lumbering in Wisconsin wasn't an active industry until the 1840s. fur trading and lead mining were still the primary sources of economic wealth. Lead miners in southwestern Wisconsin and northwestern Illinois who chose to remain through the winter months had no materials to construct suitable homes, so they were obliged to burrow caves into the hills for shelter, hence, gaining them the nickname "Badgers," a pseudonym that has remained popular among Wisconsinites to present day. When the first territorial capital building was to be erected at Belmont in 1836, there was no readily available lumber, so the necessary materials had to be shipped from Pennsylvania down the Ohio River, up the Mississippi to Galena, and then overland 25 miles by ox teams and wagons to the site of the new capitol. The scarcity of lumber held its price at a premium, and in many cases it was less expensive to have a house constructed in Pennsylvania and then transport it in sections by riverboat to Wisconsin.

Why, then, was the production of lumber so greatly delayed when there was so much available timber and even a viable means to transport it? There are a number of reasonable explanations.

Until the US Government negotiated legal possession of the land, the northern timberland rightfully belonged to the natives. It was unlawful for anyone to enter into logging operations on any Indian lands without special permission. Ironically, the government took what it needed to build military installations at Green Bay, Portage, and Prairie du Chien long before legal title was obtained, recognizing the difficulty in justifying prosecution of others cutting what they wanted. For example, in 1828 at the portage between the Fox and Wisconsin Rivers where Fort Winnebago was to be established (present-day site of Portage, Wisconsin), Second Lieutenant Jefferson Davis led a company of soldiers up the Wisconsin River to a fine tract of pine timber. They cut logs and floated them downriver to the portage where they were carted the rest of the way to the building site. There, the logs were cut into lumber with hand tools. Within two years, enough timber was cut to construct seven barracks buildings, two blockhouses, and outside of the fort proper, wash houses, commissary store, icehouse, blacksmith shop, carpenter shop, bakeshop, and stables.

Regardless of the risks of being charged with trespassing, some small scale loggers didn't wait for the land to be surveyed and sold by the government, or for the legal formalities to allow them use of the public domain. The War Department did issue permits to log on Indian land after 1830, even though the Secretary of War had no statutory right to issue such documents. These permits didn't protect the bearer from the risks, but merely assured them that the War Department wouldn't interfere with reasonable logging operations.

Another reason for the lumber industry delay in Wisconsin was the lack of investment capital. Money was in short supply in the west, and the capitalists and businessmen of the east weren't interested in pursuing such endeavors as long as the forest lands still belonged to the natives. And without the migration of skilled labor in adequate numbers, the development of the industry would have to wait for treaties to be signed.

With or without permits, sporadic logging operations were conducted in Wisconsin as early as 1810 in the areas of Green Bay, the Black River, the Chippewa River, and the Wisconsin River. These early loggers could hardly be credited with the founding of the industry, as their work wasn't of a permanent nature. But they did, however, blaze the trail to commercial lumbering for those who followed.

By 1830, immigration began to push settlers into Indian country in relatively large numbers. But the federal government had, so far, failed to remove the Indians by acquiring the pine forest lands of the Great Lakes region. Lack of sufficient building materials was hindering progress in the southern areas, as well. Then in 1832 a band of Sauk and Fox led by Chief Black Hawk threatened the rising population, resulting in the dreary event known as the Black Hawk War. Pillaging and murdering on their path northward out of Illinois into Wisconsin, they were met by the much stronger US Militia, and were soon on the run, this time in a survival attempt. The Indians were defeated in a relatively short time, and the government began negotiating treaties that provided "reservation" areas in Wisconsin, and relocated many to areas west of the Mississippi River.

The treaties that, for the most part, resolved the Indian issues produced a rush of immigrants to Wisconsin. Eastern businessmen aware of the large profits in the lumber industry of New York considered the Wisconsin woodlands a good investment. Nearly 900,000 acres of land had been purchased by settlers and speculators by the end of 1836. Excitement over this newly opened region became so great that corner building lots in some villages were selling—sight unseen—for as much as $15,000 to buyers in New York.

Despite the economic panic of 1837 that brought land speculation to an abrupt halt, the lumber industry continued to grow; it had not yet begun to meet the demand for building materials in the Mississippi Valley. Entrepreneurs who had scouted the region for tracts of timberland associated themselves with capitalists, and soon returned to the wilderness to build mills and homes and other facilities necessary to their enterprise. Most of them raised vegetables and grains for their own food and for their cattle. Before the land had been surveyed and put up for sale, a dozen or more companies were established in the territory ceded by the Winnebago and the Chippewa, and many more were forthcoming. Their shortcoming was, however, that the founders of these operations knew very little about the techniques required for running a lumbering business in the wilderness, and were quite handicapped for the lack of workers experienced in logging, manufacturing, and transporting their product. Consequently, it became necessary to import skilled managers and laborers from the older lumber communities of New Brunswick, Maine, New Hampshire, New York, and Pennsylvania. The men starting out in this new industry attracted skilled lumbermen by purchasing advertising space in New England newspapers and sent large amounts of promotional literature describing the prosperous possibilities of lumbering in the new territory, and the vast quantity of government timberland available for a nominal price. The papers informed eastern readers of the high wages paid to skilled workers, cheap lumber for building homes, prosperity to farmers who would supply the lumbermen with produce, and the success of those who had already arrived. This advertising combined with the gradual decline of lumber production in the eastern areas proved quite successful in luring skilled lumbermen to the Wisconsin pineries; they came by the hundreds. After 1840, many more came from Scandinavian countries, Germany, and Ireland. During the next fifteen years the population in the logging areas more than doubled.

Not only did this advertising attract a work force, but it also attracted numerous lumber barons from the east—men who had money to invest and to establish companies that employed the growing work force. The legislature of Wisconsin sweetened the deal by setting the legal interest rate at twelve percent. Wisconsin offered opportunities unknown in any other state in the Union.

With the great opportunities came immense difficulties, as well. It should not be surprising that more lumbering operations failed than succeeded. The task of merely penetrating into the wilderness and overcoming the seemingly insurmountable obstacles for rather meager initial earnings was discouraging. Creating a business so far removed from civilization created the problems of transporting supplies and equipment to the lumbermen. Few farmers had yet settled to produce food for the logging and mill crews; such supplies, as well as necessities like clothing, dry goods, ironwork, mill machinery and tools had to be carried by keel boats and teams over extremely difficult routes. The high transportation costs defeated many operations.

It was for this reason that some enterprising lumbermen met the problem by starting their own freighting and store business. For example, an Eau Claire logging and mill operation, Ingram, Kennedy and Company, also became a large freighting business using a custom-built steamboat that ran the Chippewa River between Read's Landing on the Mississippi and Eau Claire.

The early mills and dams were subject to nature's perils, too. Construction quality had not yet advanced, and floods often swept away everything—mill, dam, and an entire supply of logs. Adversely, low water levels due to less-than-normal snowfall during the winter meant fewer logs arriving at the mills. And fire was always an ongoing threat.

When a mill had conquered all the inherent mechanical and natural dangers of the industry, it still faced the possibility of a financial panic, as happened in 1857, and again in 1873. Markets filled to capacity as supply exceeded the demand, and lumber prices plummeted to a catastrophic level.

Despite all the pitfalls, nothing could prevent the constant growth of lumber manufacturing in Wisconsin. By 1845 it completely overshadowed fur trading and mining, and it had created a demand for agricultural products, significantly increasing the rise in that industry, as well. Lumbering in Wisconsin had unquestionably become big business when, in 1872, mills in the state produced well over a billion board feet of lumber, not including minor products such as lath and shingles. Eastern manufacturers could no longer compete with the production in Wisconsin; the market had permanently changed. Wisconsin pineries were in control of supplying building materials to the Mississippi Valley and the West.

Western expansion after the Civil War and the rapid advancement of the railroad network gave the Great Lakes region lumber trade its final and lasting boost. Speedier delivery to a nation-wide market left lumbermen only imagining what their industry would become.

LUMBER WAR

As the lumber industry expanded in Wisconsin there arose within it two conflicting interests that contributed a new chapter to the industrial history of the state. On one hand were arrayed the sawmill interests within the pineries, whose ambition was to manufacture into lumber, without interference, all the pine that was cut from the Wisconsin forests; on the other were the log driving interests whose function it was to supply raw material to the immense mills that lined the Mississippi River and the shores of Green Bay and Lake Winnebago. Nearly every important pinery stream in the state faced this conflict of interests during the period from 1857 to 1873, and the deciding clash in each case came during the decade of the sixties.

Prior to 1860 this question was nowhere regarded as important. Nearly all the logs cut in the northern forests of Wisconsin were manufactured into lumber within the pineries themselves. Perhaps a third of the small annual cut of the St. Croix and the Black was driven down the Mississippi River to supply the sawmills along its banks in Wisconsin, Iowa and Illinois. On the Chippewa River the quantity of pine disposed of in that manner was negligible; on the Wisconsin there was practically none. During the closing years of the Civil War, however, the Mississippi River mills began to lay heavier impact upon the Wisconsin forests. The alarmed sawmill owners of Wisconsin found as a result that they were obliged to pay higher prices for logs. Even more disquieting was the fact that dangerous sawmill competitors were securing a foothold in the very heart of their markets. On the Chippewa, Black and St. Croix, log driving for lower mills consumed particularly menacing proportions, and upon those streams, resulting controversies were correspondingly sharp.

The most spectacular clash occurred upon the Chippewa River, and is known as the *Beef Slough War*. This may be described in some detail, for not only was it typical of the others, but it was representative also of the standard of business ethics of the time. It foreshadowed, moreover, new developments in the lumber industry of the northwest. Out of it there arose the great lumber syndicate of its day, an organization that constituted the beginning of what became the strongest lumber power on the North American continent.

It so happened that the Chippewa River, near its mouth, divides into two channels, one of which is, for the most part, not navigable and is commonly known as Beef Slough. Beef Slough at that time formed an admirable harbor for the sorting and rafting of logs to be taken down the Mississippi River. The mill men of the Chippewa River were aware of this fact and near the close of the Civil War set about forestalling its use in any such capacity. They purchased the land at its entrance and in 1866 secured from the legislature special logging privileges there, which they had no intention of using, but only holding against possible future users.

Early in 1867 another association, consisting of prominent loggers of Michigan, Fond du Lac and Oshkosh, who had interests in the sawmills on the Mississippi River, organized a log driving association known as the *Beef Slough Manufacturing, Booming, Log Driving and Transportation Company,* and applied to the legislature for a charter to erect within Beef Slough the booms and piers necessary for their work. The bill was defeated, and immediately the victorious mill men of Eau Claire and Menomonie sent a crew of some hundreds of their employees with rafts of slabs up the entrance to the menacing slough. The logging company promptly swore out an injunction against the mill men, but not soon enough to prevent the completion of the dam. The next step that it took was more effective, however. Shrewdly dispossessing the mill men of their ownership of the head of the slough by prevailing upon friendly local authorities to condemn the land for a public highway, they forcibly tore out the offending obstruction. The latter undertaking threatened for a time to lead to a pitched battle between the opposing sawmill and the driving factions, but fortunately resulted only in a words war in rivermen's English.

Such was the status of the controversy when the legislature of 1869 convened. The logging company again made an effort to secure a charter, but its bill was decisively defeated in the assembly near the close of the session. A few days after the vote, however, an innocent appearing measure was introduced in the senate providing for the incorporation of the Portage City Gas Light Company. It was less than a week before adjournment. The bill was pushed through the legislature with the rush of business that was always present at the close of sessions, and was signed by the governor a few hours before the appointed time for adjournment.

Several days after the Portage City bill had thus become law it was learned that hidden away near its close was the following provision: "In all cases where any franchise or privilege has been or shall be granted by law to several persons, the grant shall be deemed several as well as joint, so that one or more may accept and exercise the franchise alone." The logging company had won its fight, for one of its members was a mill man who in 1866 had been associated with the Chippewa mill men as an incorporator in their unused charter. It was but a matter of form for him to assign to his new associates the rights and privileges that the secret joker in the Portage City bill had given him. The public chuckled over the sly maneuver, while the two opponents prepared for a renewal of hostilities.

Within a few months the season for the log drive from the pineries was at hand. The logging company served notice upon the mill men along the Chippewa to pass unmolested all logs bearing the Beef Slough mark. The sawmill owners were not only unwilling, but unable to do this, for only two of them possessed the necessary sorting facilities. Moreover, they were unwilling to agree upon a system of log exchanges such as had governed operations on the river until that time. Here was a deadlock, in which force again proved to be the only arbiter. The Beef Slough log drivers, numbering seventy-five rough, belligerent fellows, on their way down from the pineries were not shy to cut open whatever sawmill reservoirs they found containing any of their logs, taking from these not only their own logs but large quantities of others.

In Eau Claire County there awaited them the opposing army of the sawmill owners, numbering some 200 equally rough and determined men led by the county sheriff. As the two forces approached, the excitement and danger of a bloody clash increased. Fortunately, however, an open battle was averted. The sawmill army was too overwhelming to be resisted, and the leaders of the drive were obliged to submit to arrest. A settlement and an armed truce were eventually effected and the drivers continued on their way.

For several years after 1868, the disputes and contentions of the log driving and sawmill interests of the Chippewa River continued. In 1870 the Beef Slough Company secured from the legislature a confirmation and extension of its charter, but by this time its stormy life had brought it to bankruptcy. Its improvements were leased at the close of 1870 to an association of Mississippi River sawmill owners, among whom the leading spirit was Frederick Weyerhaeuser, the future lumber king of America. Early in 1871 this association organized the Mississippi River Logging Company, which soon became the greatest lumber syndicate of its time.

OTHER GHOSTS

OF WISCONSIN'S PAST

STANLEY EDWARD LATHROP, UNSUNG HERO

Just ten short years after the Mayflower set sail for America seeking religious freedom, the Reverend John Lathrop of England was thrown into prison for preaching his puritan views. After three years in prison, the good Reverend was released. He formed a group of followers and, in 1634, he and 42 of his flock also sailed for America. This was the beginning for the Lathrop name in America.

Moving forward in time to 1776 we find

England and America in conflict. Although the Good Reverend John Lathrop had long since made his way to Heaven, you can bet he was up there smiling. For it was his great-great-great grandson, and name sake, the Reverend John Lathrop giving the English a jab in the side. He was the minister of the *Old North Church* in Boston. And as minister, he certainly must have given his permission to use the bell tower as a beacon—*"One if by land, two if by sea."* The Lathrops went on to influence America in many ways. Six former US Presidents had Lathrop blood. A Lathrop served on the Supreme Court. And as you will see, a Nineteenth Century member of the Lathrop clan made a very profound and lasting impact on American society.

Stanley Lathrop was born May 7, 1843 in Orville, New York. He was the son of Congregational minister Alfred Crafts Lathrop. Alfred Lathrop was eight generations apart from the Reverend that came from England, but he shared the same love of God and puritan views of his forefathers. These views were passed on to young Stanley.

Stanley was just ten years old when the Lathrop's moved from New York to the wilderness of Wisconsin, coming first by steamer to

Sheboygan, and then by stagecoach to Neenah, where they stayed one year before finally settling in New London. It was here that Reverend Lathrop spent many years preaching the Congregational ways, including abolition, at numerous churches throughout the area.

It was here that young Stanley grew up. At age thirteen, Stanley went to work at the local newspaper office, where he learned a trade that he used throughout much of the rest of his life. He was the "Printer's Devil." At that time, print type consisted of individual letters and numbers carved on wooden blocks. Once the editor wrote the stories, it was the Printer's Devil's job to arrange the blocks on the press for the pages to be printed. Stanley excelled at his job, just as he did in school and in his religious studies. Stanley went on to study at Ripon College, and then Beloit College to become a minister, following in this father's footsteps. It was there at Beloit College that his story really begins. The Civil War broke out in 1861 and the call went out for soldiers for the Union Army. Young men were enlisting all around Stanley. By the following letter he penned to his father, it is quite evident that he, too, was willing and eager to fight for his Country.

Beloit College, April 21, 1861.

Dear Father:

I write to obtain your consent to enlist, as I am not yet eighteen years of age. Since I wrote you, some stirring events have transpired in this country. A few days ago, Fort Sumpter [sic] was in possession of the Federal government, and the glorious old stars and stripes were proudly floating over its battlements. Now it stands a blackened ruin, made so by the traitorous guns of the Southern Confederacy. This is the finishing stroke to a long catalogue of injuries and insults. It is now reported that these rebels are marching upon our national capital, with the professed purpose to wrest the government from our hands, and in its place set up one whose root and foundation is that abomination of abominations, Slavery! It is not enough to make every free man and lover of liberty spring to arms, and to make every drop of blood in our throbbing hearts swell with indignation? When we see the glorious flag of our Union, and the same old banner under which our ancestors fought and bled, torn ignominiously from its place, trampled in the dust, and supplanted by the detestable rattlesnake flag of South Carolina, it is enough to make every patriot gird on the "sword of the Lord and of Gideon," and go willingly to fight the battles of his country and his God. This is why I wish to go and give my services to my country; for, as President Chapin said the other night, to the volunteers in Beloit, "We know that our country is right." I believe that the "irrepressible conflict" between right and wrong, truth and error, freedom and slavery, has come, and I want to help on the side of truth.

I never in my life saw anything like the excitement and enthusiasm which appeared here at the reception of President Lincoln's proclamation calling for 75,000 men. The days of '76 are again revived. There are no democrats or republicans here now - nothing but patriots. Men who but a few days ago were engaged in the bitterest political disputes, are now as a band of brothers, doing all that in them lies for the cause of their country. There was a union meeting held in Hackett Hall on Wednesday night which was attended by hundreds. Democrats and republicans, students and merchants, ministers and laymen, made patriotic speeches. Among the best speakers were Dr. Brinsmade, pastor of the First Congregational church, Mr. Graves, pastor of the Second Congregational church, and others. The enthusiasm was thrilling. A paper being opened for the names of volunteers, seventeen of the best young men of the town came forward and signed, among whom were some of our most earnest Christian students. The meeting was adjourned till Friday evening. Speeches were made at that time by President Chapin, Senator Bennett, and others of our most distinguished men. Several students spoke, offering themselves as volunteers, amid the wildest excitement.

State Senator Bennett said the legislature had just adjourned, after having given the governor $200,000 for the war and five times as much if needed. The legislature also had suspended specie payment of the solvent banks in the state until December, passed a bill to exempt from civil process the property of volunteers, another to protect their families, etc. Quite a number of students enlisted that night, besides others. The full number for a company (78 men) is more than secured already. The city will furnish them with arms, ammunition, uniforms, etc. Governor Randall telegraphed that two regiments are already filled, and two or three more will be needed.

The students bought and raised a large flag over Middle college yesterday. Speeches were made by President Chapin, Professors Porter, Kelsey and several students. It is useless trying to study amid such exciting scenes. Nobody can do it. Quite a number of new students lately arrived, and several enlisted as soon as they could. Two ex-army officers here have offered their services in drilling us. We have formed a company of students and shall begin drilling at once. If President Lincoln issues another call for troops, we shall offer our services to Governor Randall, and if accepted, go immediately into service. President Chapin said in his Sunday afternoon lecture, "It may be that the great battle of Armageddon is at hand; and we must be ready, as Christians and as men, to take our places in the struggle." Professor Blaisdell also has made some stirring speeches.

That our dear country may be delivered from slavery and from all its evils, is the prayer of

Your Affectionate Son,
Stanley E. Lathrop.

Two days later, on April 23rd, Stanley wrote his father again, this time to say that he could wait no longer and that he had enlisted. They would be marching to Camp Randall in Madison soon. Thus began the 20,000 mile journey of Chaplin Stanley Lathrop and Wisconsin's Iron brigade – the 1ST

Calvary, a journey that included no less than 54 enemy engagements and culminated in the capture of Jefferson Davis. Lathrop's war records indicate he was active in 48 engagements. Having been captured twice, and then mustered out of the Calvary for several months due to injuries, must have kept Stanley from being there for every battle.

In the following article from the *Eau Claire Leader*, March 16, 1906, Stanley relates a sampling of his military experiences:

> *In 1862 my regiment made a raid into Arkansas, fighting every day and capturing many prisoners. One day we took a little town after a sharp skirmish, and when we had more prisoners than we had men in our regiment. The Colonel deciding to parole the prisoners detailed me and another soldier printer boy to print blank paroles as soon as possible. The local editor had deserted his little printing office and we took possession. With the old fashioned rude materials we printed the needed paroles on a scorching July day. The*

prisoners gladly signed the paroles and went gladly on their way rejoicing.

A few days after a small detachment of us were surrounded by a regiment of Texas rangers and after a fight in which we lost three-fourths of our men, a few of us were captured. We were taken to Little Rock and confined sixteen men in one small room. We asked for something to read but this was refused. Then we organized the "Y.J.B.R.C." which being interpreted means "The Yankee Jail Birds Reading Club". We had neither book nor paper to read. But one member was appointed to repeat what he could remember, for example of Robinson Crusoe, the audience listening criticizing and correcting. Next day another would recite from Hamlet, Julius Caesar, or the Shakespearean plays. Then perhaps Scott's Ivanhoe Rob Roy or Midlothian: then Dickens, Thackeray, or other less famous writers. I even did what few printers have ever done, taught the printer's art in prison. Drawing the outline of a type case on the floor with charcoal and marking the boxes, upper and lower case, we borrowed a jack-knife and whittled out wooden type from a piece of bellywood brought by one of our good natured guards who was curious to see what "them Yanks" could do. We whittled out a "printer's stick" from a piece of board. So I taught the rudiments to some of the boys. Three of them after the war became prosperous printers and publishers.

Another newspaper article recounts further experience of this time period:

"You see, it was mid October 1862. I had been taken prisoner of war in Arkansas, paroled and sent to St. Louis from Little Rock on 'Shank's horses'. All Wisconsin paroled prisoners were sent via Mississippi steamer to old Fort Crawford at Prairie Du Chien where some of us

were furloughed and sent home I had railroad transportation to Madison, where I decided to make a bee line to my old home in Westfield, 60 miles North. I started northward on foot, carrying knapsack, overcoat and blanket. Weakened by strenuous campaigning, imprisonment, poor food, chills and fever. I made slow progress. And the miles seemed very long. At last I reached Token Creek, ten miles north, utterly exhausted. Having no pay for six months I was penniless. Telling my story to the kind-hearted Token Creek landlord of a little tavern, he was very sympathetic – fed me on the (chicken) fat of the land, and put me to bed where I slept most refreshingly. Starting out next morning with the landlord's breakfast and blessing, I resumed the homeward march. I cannot remember the landlord's name, but I heard later that he raised a company and went to war. Traveling in the teeth of a sharp, cold north wind, I trudged on mile after mile, getting a ride for several miles with an old farmer whose son was in the war down south. There was no railroad to Portage then. Late that night I reached Portage, where another patriotic landlord gave me bed and board, refusing my offer to pay him when I arrived home."

At this time, Stanley Lathrop was mustered out of the 1st Cavalry due to weakened state and disability. The discharge was dated January 10, 1863. Eleven months later, fully recovered, he re-enlisted with Wisconsin's 1st Cavalry and remained until July 19, 1865, just after the capture of Jeff Davis. During his army career, he was a war correspondent for several Wisconsin newspapers, and served as a military job printer under General John C. Fremont in Missouri and Arkansas, under Rosenerans, Grant, and Thomas in Tennessee, and under "Uncle Billy Sherman" in Mississippi, Alabama, Georgia and Florida.

After discharge from the Union Army, Lathrop returned to his home state of Wisconsin, re-entered Beloit College and was graduated in 1867.

The following fall, he enrolled at the Chicago Theological Seminary.

The year 1870 was quite eventful for Stanley Lathrop: he graduated from the Seminary and was ordained; he married Elizabeth Littlell of Tomah, Wisconsin; he became the minister of a church in Viroqua, Wisconsin, where he stayed for two years. Then, his calling found him as the minister at his father's church in New London.

Six years later, The American Missionary Association sent him as a missionary to Macon, Georgia. They provided him with a church and a school; he was both pastor and principal. He soon learned that no Negro could draw a book from the public library, so, with the help of friends in the North, he secured a printing press and started a little paper called *The Helping Hand*, taking its title from the motto of Edward Everett Hale, "Look up and not down, look out and not in, and lend a hand." He called his newspaper "a little sheet meant to do good," and by the circulation of his paper, on which he did all the composition and press work, he established the first free library for colored people in the whole South, with contributions of books coming from Henry Ward Beecher, Edward Evertt Hale, George W. Cable,

Harriett Beecher Stowe, Mark Twain, his old commander, General Wilson, and a number of leading Southerners as Gen. John B. Gordon and Gov. Joe Brown. White people of Macon gave money for the small library building, in the basement of which was established one of the earliest industrial schools for Negroes in the South. In 1928 the library had 6,000 volumes and was still providing service.

Realizing the destitute condition of the freedmen both in poverty and in mentality, Lathrop strove to help them in body, mind, and spirit. He spread good books, magazines and papers far and wide, and clothing for the needy, received from friends all over the country. The humble beginning of industrial education for the Negroes received generous aid from Mr. Stephen Ballard, so that a separate building for this purpose was erected. Pupils were taught how to build houses and earn good wages as mechanics. Lathrop's wife conducted sewing classes for the women, and at times there were three generations from one family learning to sew garments.

Then came four years of service among the mountain whites, where, in a valley in the Cumberland Mountains, Lathrop strove to bring the light of the gospel and of education among a people ignorant and superstitious. None of the adults could read or write, nor could few of the children. A school, Sherwood Academy, had been established for them, but they resented any idea of progress, and there were times when Lathrop's life was in real danger. Ashamed for their lack of clothes suitable for church, he carried the church to them by holding meetings in the little one-room cabins on the mountainside, where the only light was tallow candles and the kerosene lantern he carried. Many an evening he climbed up steep paths, leading his oldest daughter by the hand, crossing deep mountain canyons on a foot log, and at times carrying his daughter in one arm and the lantern in the other, while the water roared below. The little girl was always a sweet singer and was of great assistance in singing the gospel message in those lonely cabins. In this valley another library was founded of 2400 volumes through the agency of *The Helping Hand.* Here again sewing meetings were held by his faithful helpmate, and the daughter would sing to these humble folk.

After several months of lecturing in New England on his work in the South, Lathrop was promoted to the office of State Superintendent of the American Missionary Association in Texas, but after one year of being almost always away from his home which was so dear to him, he resigned and brought his family back to Wisconsin, where he performed missionary work in the northern part of the state, in one place building a parsonage, and also building two new churches in pioneer communities. Here again he distributed books, magazines and papers everywhere, and founded the *North Wisconsin Traveling Library Association* which sent libraries into many isolated communities and lumber camps. One saloon keeper complained because his business was being ruined when the lumbermen stayed in camp on Sunday and read from the books and papers sent to them instead of drinking and gambling in his saloon.

Lathrop became interested in North Wisconsin Academy and eventually became its traveling agent, raising money, books, students, and friends for its support. This academy developed into Northland College of Ashland, Wisconsin.

The academy had a debt of $18,000 and one building, but at a meeting of its friends, when he was receiving a salary of only $700 with a family of six children to support, he made a liberal subscription, causing considerable sacrifice to him and his family. On such sacrifices Northland College was made possible. His little paper was again busy, asking for books and papers and help for the struggling school.

After Ashland, Lathrop went to Madison to become the State Chaplin for the Grand Army of the Republic (G.A.R.), and in 1915 he became the tour guide for the newly built State Capitol, and wrote its guide book in intricate detail.

In his lifetime over 100,000 books and millions of magazines and papers, and innumerable Bibles and Testaments were given in the South and North, spreading cheer and uplift to plantations, country schools, city slums, penitentiaries, convicts, miners, river boatmen, factory hands, veterans of the Union and Confederate homes, mountaineers, lumbermen, boarding houses, and many others. It is a conservative estimate that at one time or another during his ministry as a soldier of the Cross, over 15,000,000 people were supplied with wholesome and inspiring reading.

Stanley Edward Lathrop called Wisconsin his home. He is truly an unsung hero whose labors have gone unnoticed until now. He never had more than a few dollars in his pocket, but it was the fire and conviction in his heart, to serve God, Country, and his fellow man that sets this gentleman apart.

FIRST BREWERY IN LA CROSSE

The rise of the brewing industry in La Crosse, Wisconsin pre-dates the Civil War and Victorian periods in the history of the city. It developed into what became one of the city's leading industries.

John Gund Sr. came to La Crosse in 1854, just thirteen years after Nathan Myrick first settled on Barron's Island. (Pettibone) He found La Crosse to be not much more than a trading post. But settlers were pouring in into this new territory every month. With the prospect of a growing population, Gund took up one of his two trades that he knew best—brewing.

Gund was born October 3, 1830 at Schwetzingen, a small village in Germany. His father, George Gund, was a hop and tobacco farmer. John learned two trades—cooperage and brewing. After his parents left for United States in

1847 he continued working in Germany for a year. At the age of 18 he sailed for New York, and then traveled to Freeport, Illinois where his parents had located.

From Freeport he went to Galena, Illinois, and then to Dubuque, Iowa where he worked in the brewery there, but he soon returned to Galena to become involved with the operations of two breweries. Four years later he went to La Crosse and built his own brewery.

That first brewery was housed in a small log building on the southeast corner of what is now Front and Division Streets. Mr. Gund believed that a brewery should be located at the edge of the city, and outside the city limits. He chose that location because, at the time, La Crosse was comprised of only a handful of structures. For the same reason, in later years, he erected is new plant on the prairie land that is now along South Avenue.

Gund's first year of business in La Crosse was on a very small scale compared to the production of his Empire Brewery a half-century later. In that first year his output was 500 barrels of beer, with only a dozen men working for him. Fifty years later, his Empire Brewery employed several hundred.

For four long years Gund worked at his trade in his own brewery, but in 1858 he went into partnership with Gottlieb Heileman, building and opening the City Brewery, later to be known as the G. Heileman Brewery.

But Gund was not without competition; another brewer, Frederick Defengaber, made a bold effort to establish his business in 1856. But the antiquated machinery used in that brewery was never upgraded, and prevented any progress. History records that Defengaber left the city in 1870. Two years after the competing brewery had closed, John Gund branched out; in 1872 he dissolved partnership with Mr. Heileman and built the Empire Brewery on South Avenue.

Also, about 1856, a Dr. Nicolai began brewing beer in a small building at what is now Second and Pearl Streets. A year later, Charles and John Michel opened the first brewery of any size in La Crosse at Third and Division Streets; their first year of business yielded 1,000 barrels of lager beer.

In those early days the method and process of brewing was naturally crude and uncultured as compared with the scientific art of brewing as it was eventually mastered. At that time, the workmen usually had their sleeping quarters in the brewery, working twelve- eighteen-hour days. All work was done by hand, the operations being naturally slow and tedious. For instance, the cleansing of kegs and bottles was done in a most primitive manner. Pitch heated to a liquid form was poured into a keg and the keg was then rolled back and forth. In later years the kegs were cleansed, inspected, pre-heated, and pitched in one operation by means of more modern machinery.

When brewers began to produce bottled beer, a small quantity of lead shot was placed in each bottle, which was shaken by hand for the purpose of loosening any particles of dirt in the bottle. Subsequently they were rinsed out in water in the same crude way. Each bottle was handled separately in this process of cleaning, pasteurizing, and labeling. With "modern" equipment the bottles were placed in a soaker machine, automatically passing through a caustic solution and on to the automatic brushing machine. Later they went through the pasteurizer. Labeling machines attached the gummed paper labels to the bottles.

Refrigeration was not known in those early days, yet the beer had to be dept cool. As a consequence, the beer was made in the winter months and hauled by sleighs to the bluffs along the Mormon Coulee Road where large caves had been dug into the cliffs. The beer was pumped from the kegs into large wooden tanks in the caves; there the beer was stored and retrieved as needed during the summer. Many a story was told of the days when large bobsleds carted great loads of beer kegs to these caves, overturning on the way, sending the full kegs rolling merrily down the hillside.

At the time the Civil War began, there were just four breweries in operation in La Crosse. In most cases, they were but humble beginnings of what in later years were to develop into a great industry. The Civil War years saw little progress, but during the reconstruction period that followed, the brewing business again began to boom. New breweries opened and the older firms started to expand. However, many of the smaller firms did not survive the last half of the Nineteenth Century.

The period from the Civil War to 1890 was most important in the development of the industry, however, not until the advent of the "machine age" of the Twentieth Century and the introduction of refrigeration did beer production reach its maximum. Of the four breweries operating in La Crosse at the outbreak of the Civil War, it is estimated that the total production was not more than 25,000 barrels per year. There are several reasons why production was not so great in those early years. First, the breweries operated only during the winter; lacking the means of refrigeration, they could only manufacture the beer in the cold weather, and store it in the bluff caves. Although the exact date is not known, it was sometime in the early 1860s that the La Crosse breweries first began using river ice for refrigeration. Storage houses were built by all the active brewers. Ice refrigeration was a great step forward. European brewers laughed at American tradesmen when they told their counterparts in the old country of the new method of storing beer. They said it couldn't be done, and they clung to the age-old method of letting nature provide the cooling facilities deep in the earth.

Another reason that production in that time period remained low was the lack of effective transportation. None of the local breweries had much of an outside market. That development—in great proportions—was yet to come.

Lack of machinery to do the most exacting

tasks in the brewery was another reason for low production. All the work had to be done by hand; bottled beer was almost unheard of at that time. All beer was put up in wooden casks. Those breweries not having their own cooperage departments contracted local cooperage shops to make their casks for them, which in itself was another industry of that age.

Brewers of the Civil War era experienced a difficult time to survive the war period. The government placed a heavy tax of one dollar per barrel on all beer produced as an emergency measure, with a promise that it would not last much more than a year. But after three years it still remained. It was finally reduced to fifty cents per barrel by an act of congress.

With an investment of $25,000 at the close of the War, George Zeisler and Otto Nagel erected a three-story stone building along Third Street, and started the brewery that was later known as George Zeisler and Sons. First year production was 1,000 barrels. Two years later, Mr. Zeisler became sole owner of the business. His production increased in the next five years, demanding expansion and improvements to the plant. Then, in December, 1873 the structure caught fire and burned to the ground. Reconstruction began, and with plans of re-opening on July 4, 1874, the new plant caught on fire, but was only partially destroyed. The buildings were fully insured, so Zeisler suffered only the loss of time and consequent business. He rebuilt again, this time a four-story brick and stone structure at a cost of $35,000. Eight men were employed in the brewery at the time of re-opening, and 3,200 barrels of beer were produced each year. The John Gund Brewing Company bought the Zeisler brewery in 1902, a few months following George Zeisler's death.

John Gund dissolved his partnership with Gottlieb Heileman in the City Brewery in 1872, and the next year began construction of the Empire Brewing Company at Ninth Street and South Avenue, then only open prairie land. At the start, the Gund plant was only a small one, though much larger than his first brewery at Front and Division Streets. Over the years, it was practically rebuilt and received extensive additions to the extent that it might easily have been considered a completely new plant. His investment prior to 1890 was $250,000.

The enlarged brewery employed about 25 men in 1880. The use of ice for refrigeration made possible the expansion and it grew to such an extent that before 1880 the plant had two ice houses, one of which called for 1,300 tons of ice in the overhead ice room.

Ice houses of that time consisted of a basement, main floor, and an overhead ice room. Both basement and main floors were used for storage; they contained many great hogsheads of beer, each of which contained about 35-40 barrels, a barrel being 31 gallons. The ice buildings were well insulated and usually were connected with the brewing house, making convenient transportation of the new brew to the storage facility.

There is not much to be said about the growth of the G. Heileman Brewery in the early years following the Civil War. It is known that in 1860 when John Gund was still associated with the firm, 500 barrels of beer were produced per year. When he withdrew from the business, production had increased to 3,000 barrels annually.

Mr. Heileman died in 1878, but his wife continued to operate the business under the same company name for some time. The business continued to grow; 7,170 barrels of beer were produced in 1880; twelve men and three boys were employed. E.T. Mueller became the plant manager in 1884; he was Mr. Heileman's son-in-law.

The G. Heileman Brewing Company operated until nearly the end of the Twentieth Century.

The Eagle Brewery opened at Twelfth and La Crosse Streets the same year that Zeisler and Nagel started the brewery on North Third Street. This property changed hands several times in the next few years. It became known as the Franz Bartl Brewery in 1886. Production capacity increased at this brewery from 1,000 barrels in 1867 to about 10,000 in 1890.

The only known brewery to be operated in North La Crosse was the Voegele Brewery, later to be Erickson's or Monitor Brewery; its location was on Monitor Street at Copeland Avenue. John Erickson gained possession in 1898 and ran it until 1923.

WISCONSIN STREET CARS

There was a time when, in the larger Wisconsin cities, street cars operated on railway systems. As populations grew, the need arose for mass-transit. The typical car, drawn by one or two horses, could comfortably accommodate 25-30 passengers.

Col. George H. Walker opened the first street railway to the public in Milwaukee in 1860; by 1882 in that city, three rail companies operated, each in different sections of the metropolis, a combined total of about 40 cars daily.

All the earliest cars were open; in cold weather, the drivers were muffled in buffalo coats, and the floor was covered with hay to add a little passenger "comfort." Only two lanterns on each coach provided light, one at the fare box behind the driver, and one at the rear. It was a one-man operation, the driver taking care of the fare box and the passengers, as well as tending the horses. During daytime hours, each car was propelled with two horses, but during the evening rush, three were used. Drivers earned 13 cents an hour.

The heaviest traffic occurred on Sundays; it was considered in vogue to ride a trolley to Schlitz Park or the beach, where entire families would go to spend the day.

When electrification of the street car systems began in 1890, the horses and cars were replaced by larger, speedier, motor-driven coaches. By then, the railways had been extended to provide service to a much greater area. Eventually, the tree companies merged into one, which also acquired an independent line to Waukesha.

The new company donated one of the old horse cars to the teachers of the Sixth District school who were in the habit of taking their pupils on weekend outings to Waukesha Beach. The retired car was set up on the wilderness beach and was used for many years as a shelter and headquarters for these jaunts.

That oldest remaining horse-drawn Milwaukee street car was given one last commemorative trip on the streets in 1921. It was mounted on wheels and brought back to the city for Milwaukee's Diamond Jubilee parade. However, it was later dismantled, a relic of the past relegated to the oblivion of lost treasures.

The network of street railway lines in La Crosse that remained in service into the mid-twentieth century was the outgrowth of a horse-drawn system that originated in 1879, extending from Third and Main in downtown to Windsor Street on the north side.

In the spring of that year, David Law and Michael Funk conceived the idea of organizing what was known as the *La Crosse Street Railway Company* for the purpose of providing passenger transportation service between the north and south sides of the city. The principal industry on the north side was lumber, eight or more saw mills being located on that side of the La Crosse River. Many of the north side mill employees lived in the south side; a plank road connected the two sides of the city, but there were no means of public transportation to get them to and from their work.

The announcement that La Crosse would have a street car line was received with general approval, however, construction of a bridge and laying tracks over the La Crosse River came in question. For a time, it appeared as though this objection might block the project. But one Sunday morning a crew of men was put to work on the job and the line was completed before Monday morning, thus avoiding injunction proceedings. The bridge structure remained and was in service for many years. The company constructed a car barn at Mill and Car Streets where its horses and six small cars were housed.

The Street Railway connected the north and south sides; the fare was five cents; it was well patronized right from the start, and in a short time the line on the north side was extended to Logan Street. This extension proved to be profitable, and in 1888 the company decided to again extend the line still farther north. That part of the city had expanded as a result of the *Chicago-Burlington & Northern Railway* building through La Crosse on its route between Chicago and Minneapolis. The street car line extension accommodated the large number of employees at the Burlington shops and roundhouse.

About the same time, another street car line was organized, known as the *La Crosse City Railway Company*. This system ran south from the Milwaukee Railroad Depot located in downtown La Crosse (Second and Vine Streets) to Gund's Brewery on Mormon Coulee Road, where the car barn was built.

The two lines were operated independently for several years, but eventually consolidated under the name La *Crosse Street Railway Company*. Further expansion provided transportation service south and east from the downtown area, and when the La Crosse Interstate Fair was organized in 1890, the line was extended to the fairgrounds entrance.

With the extensions, more rolling stock was added until the company owned 19 horse cars. Most of them were drawn by a single horse, each one carrying a bell so the approaching street car could be heard. The front platforms were unprotected from the elements; during winter weather, the drivers wore heavy fur coats, and hay on the floor protected against the cold. The cars were lighted with kerosene lamps, but there were no stoves for heat; windows became coated with thick layers of frost, making it necessary for the passengers to scrape a peep hole to see when they were nearing their destination. During daytime operation, cars ran at ten-minute intervals, each making a round trip in about an hour. After 8:00 PM, the number of cars was reduced.

Although the cars were small, seats ordinarily accommodated 30 passengers. On special occasions, however, as many as 50 people crowded into each car. At these times, two horses were used to power the overloaded coaches.

One of the difficulties encountered with horse cars was their jumping off the tracks, which was a common occurrence. So often did it happen that the passengers willingly assisted in getting the car back on the track rather than suffering a long delay in reaching their destination.

The La Crosse Street Railway system was electrified in 1893, beginning with the first cars operating over the north side line, but before winter set in, the entire city system was equipped with electric cars, the electricity generated at the power station at the corner of Third and La Crosse Streets. The first electrified cars were built by combining two of the old horse cars. One of them—known as "Long Annie," was in service for many years, but over all, this experiment proved unworthy, as the old horse cars were too frail to withstand the heavier loads and rougher use to which they were subjected, and that idea was soon abandoned. The old horse cars were relegated to use as trailers during special occasions.

The new *Orange Line* buses that appeared in Janesville July, 1929 caused quite a stir, however, exactly 43 years earlier, more excitement erupted over the new street car line.

The first trip over the street railway in Janesville was made on July 22, 1886, as car No. 1 was placed on the tracks at the railroad crossing on Academy Street at 8:30 AM. Only the company officers and two or three citizens were allowed to board, as the car was only to be run over the road for the purpose of an inspection. After a brief stop near the Commercial Hotel to repair a harness, the car continued on to the "end of the line" at Pearl and Washington Streets. Then it proceeded to the opposite "end of the line" across the Milwaukee Street Bridge to North Main. It attracted considerable attention all along the route; it was, of course, the first street car to appear in the city, and quite a curiosity to many.

The tracks were deemed in very good condition, and the passengers on board were quite pleased with the opportunity to be the first to ride a Janesville street car.

These cars were considerably smaller than those used in the bigger cities, attractively painted white with yellow panels; numbers and the words "Janesville Street Railway" over the windows in silver leaf. The insides were finished in the color of natural maple and ash wood. Glass transoms and ventilators provided an ample supply of fresh air. Five strong, well-built horses were bought for use on the railway, and all were quite capable of taking a loaded car from one end of the line to the other without trouble. However, when the line was extended to the fairgrounds, an extra horse was used for assistance with loaded cars up the steep grade to East Milwaukee Street.

Advancement in the design of motor cars, making them more useable year-round, perhaps was the beginning of the street car decline in Wisconsin in the 1930s. Most were gone by the mid-1900s. But what a grand piece of history they added to Wisconsin's past!

APPLETON LIGHTS & ELECTRIC RAILWAY

Although it wasn't the first in the United States, Appleton, Wisconsin can be credited with the first electric generating plant in the West, providing electricity for the general public.

For quite some time, Thomas Edison had been developing the incandescent electric light and the equipment to supply the power. His system was tested in several private homes; then a central power station was put into service at Menlo Park, New Jersey in the winter of 1881-82 for demonstration purposes, but not until late 1882 was it available for public use.

The system had been tried in London, but was unsuccessful as a permanent installation. In the United States, however, the Edison Electric

Illuminating Company of New York, organized in 1880, was busy laying the plans for a means of lighting the city with electricity, using the Edison central station system. Property on Pearl Street in New York was acquired and work began laying the underground conductors, but it would be September 4, 1882 when the Pearl Street station was put into operation.

During this same time period, the Western Edison Electric Light Company of Chicago was incorporated, and acquired territorial rights for Illinois, Wisconsin, and Iowa. Edison's electric lighting system was placed on the Western market in May 1882.

By July that year, the Chicago company had attracted the interest of a group of mill owners and other citizens of Appleton, Wisconsin; they were eager to experiment with the new lighting system, and they would soon make their city noteworthy in electricity history.

Led by H.J. Rogers, president of the Appleton Paper and Pulp Company, the group invited an engineer of the Western Edison Light Company to Appleton to explain the new system to the group of businessmen. They became quite intrigued by the possibilities of lighting their mills and their homes with electricity, and they were hopeful of making this "invisible power" available to the general public, as well.

Edison's engineer satisfied the Appleton investors; they contracted the Western Edison Light Company in mid-August to supply them with two water power driven Edison "K" dynamos with the capability to light 550 lamps. Sometime later, a construction man/ electrician was sent from Chicago to install the first generator at the paper company's mill. Installation took nearly six weeks; although it was not the first in the US, the Appleton system was the earliest use of a central station power plant in the West, and the first to be driven by water power. This mill and another mill a mile away, both owned by Appleton Paper and Pulp, as well as the newly constructed residence of Company President Rogers were wired.

There were rumors about this time that Mr. Rogers, who was also the president of the local gas company, had purchased the rights to the electric lighting system merely to keep it from competing with the gas business, and that he never intended to make it a public utility. On September 9, 1882, the *Appleton Crescent* newspaper disproved the rumors, reporting the wiring process at the mills and Rogers' home, and "if it proves an unquestioned success, as of course it cannot fail to, then the light will be substituted generally for gas in all our public and private buildings and the gas will be cheapened, used for heating, cooking, and running light machinery." Certainly, the businessmen who initiated the project were truly prophets and believers in American inventiveness.

Late September, the same newspaper announced that the mills would undergo a test of the new lighting system, and on Wednesday the 27th, all was ready, however, when the power was applied, the lights failed to glow. It was assumed that the failure was due to the high moisture caused by the steam from the mill. The Edison engineer was summoned from Chicago by telegraph; he quickly discovered some slight errors in the wiring arrangements, which were easily corrected. Saturday September 30, 1882, the dynamo was put into operation, and the hanging pear-shaped globes emitted the incredible, steady incandescent light. Observers declared the illuminated buildings to be "bright as day." The experiment was a great success; the confidence of the mill owners had been justified.

The test was then repeated at the Rogers

residence with gratifying success; it was the first home in the West to be exclusively lighted by the Edison system.

As with the trial of any new mechanical system, problems did arise. The waterwheel used to drive the dynamo also drove some new machinery in the mill. Because of the varying load on the machines, so did the waterwheel and dynamo speed greatly vary. Sometimes the voltage rose so high that all the lamps in the circuit were burned out. After several of these incidents, the dynamo was moved to another location in the mill, and was driven by its own waterwheel.

The second dynamo of the contract was originally installed in the Vulcan mill at the opposite side of the city. The owners decided, however, to construct a building independent of the two mills at a point between them. The dynamos were then transferred to that location, and the quickly-erected frame shack became the first central station for commercial electricity production in the West, the predecessor of all the great generating plants that we know today. By December 1882, several more residences, the Appleton Blast Furnace, A.W. Patten's Paper Mill, Fleming's Linen Mill, and the Appleton Woolen Mill were all illuminated by Edison lights. The following January, lights were successfully installed in the Waverly Hotel, giving great satisfaction. The local newspaper boasted that Appleton then had more electrically lighted buildings than any other city in the United States.

Service was from dusk to daylight only; there were no meters to measure the usage of electricity, so patrons of the light utility paid a flat rate of $1.20 per month per lamp for all-night service. If used only until ten o'clock p.m., the rate was eighty-four cents per month. All customers purchased their own lamps at a cost of $1.60 each.

Because there was no fuse protection, the bare copper power lines were subject to short circuits, causing occasional power failure to the entire system. Wind, or anything out of the ordinary like a branch falling off a tree, if it fell against the wires, would create a short circuit, and the system would have to be shut down. All company hands then went out to find where the trouble was; sometimes it took an hour, sometimes a day, and in the meantime, there was no service.

By the 1920s, the Appleton Edison Light Company supplied electric service to fourteen surrounding municipalities and villages, and operated power lines over an area of more than fifty square miles.

Electric Railway

Not many people know that the electric railway had its start in Appleton, Wisconsin. F.E. Harriman, an Appleton real estate operator, instituted the first electric railway there in 1887. Constructed from east to west city limits traversing the main business area, it operated along that same route well into the Twentieth Century.

The proposed project was received with great skepticism, endless debate over its usefulness, and whether operating heavy cars with the invisible electric power could even be accomplished. The doubters were in large majority; failure was freely predicted. The promoter—Harriman—was looked upon as a dreamer and a visionary, but he maintained vigilant attention to the task until construction of the line was completed and the rolling stock arrived.

The announcement was made that power would be turned on and the cars would operate, the trial run commencing at the extreme east end of the line where there was a steep hill. A car was placed on the track, and the public was invited to witness the beginning of this new era.

Half of the population turned out to observe what they expected to be a failed venture; scoffers laughed at the presumption of anyone who believed sufficient power could be sent over a small copper wire to propel a heavy, loaded car up the hill.

A sufficient number of people from the assembled crowd were requested to board the car to take a free ride. The car was filled, and many even clung to the outside wherever footing could be secured. It was a crucial moment. Success or failure was imminent. Absolute silence prevailed. The crowd seemed to hold its breath.

The promoter, who envisioned great things from this, stood courageously beside the car. He raised his hand and gave the signal. Power was turned on by the motorman and the heavily loaded car jerked forward, slowly at first, and then gradually gained speed as it started off on the first journey ever made by an electrically propelled vehicle.

At that moment, a great industry was born that soon would become widespread across the country, and it would remain a pillar in transportation for many years to come. By 1922, in Wisconsin alone, more than 260,000,000 passengers had ridden the urban electric railways.

References and Sources:

In addition to countless personal visits to the many towns, cities, and historical sites named in this book, the following is a list of information sources.   (Listed in no particular order.)

Special thanks to my long-time friend, Eric Leum, for his input for the Springville story and for supplying the vintage cover photo of "Old Town." Also, thanks to Ron Nagel who supplied the research for stories about Paul Seifert and Edward Lathrop.

Various historical markers in Wisconsin.

Organizations and websites: Wisconsin State Historical Society; La Crosse County (Wisconsin) Historical Society; Portage (Wisconsin) Public Library; La Crosse (Wisconsin) Public Library; Mid-Continent Railroad Museum at North Freedom, Wisconsin; Middleton (Wisconsin) Public Library; Chippewa County Historical Society; Wisconsin Department of Natural Resources; Juneau County Historical Society; Rock County Historical Society; Grant County Historical Society; Monroe County Historical Society; Pepin County Historical Society; Richland County Historical Society; First Capitol website; Blue Mounds Village Hall

Newspaper archives: La Crosse Tribune; Milwaukee Sentinel; Milwaukee Journal; Viroqua Censor; Wisconsin

State Journal (Madison); Portage Democrat; Eau Claire Leader; Westby Times; The Muscoda Democrat; La Crosse Leader; Eau Claire Daily Telegram; Dunn County News; Chicago Herald; Chippewa Falls Independent;   La Crosse Chronicle; Baraboo Weekly News; Milwaukee Free Press; Burlington Hawkeye; Janesville Gazette; Beloit Daily News; Madison Democrat; Racine Times-Call; Mauston Chronicle; Mount Horeb Times; Prairie du Chien Press; Lancaster Herald; Monroe Evening Times; The Chicago Tribune; Belmont Gazette; Chippewa Falls Herald; Manitowoc Herald; Fennimore Times; Weekly Home News (Spring Green, Wisconsin)

Other publications: *History of Northern Wisconsin, 1881*; *Stagecoach and Tavern Tales of the Old Northwest* by Harry E. Cole; *West Central Wisconsin History*, Vol. 1 & 2; *Chapters in the History of Richland County, Wisconsin* by Margaret Helen Scott; *Cyclopedia of Wisconsin* edited by Ex-Gov. George W. Peck; *Julien's Journal—The Dubuque Area Magazine; The Wisconsin River* by Richard Durbin; *Wisconsin Historical Collections; Wisconsin Magazine of History*

ABOUT THE AUTHOR

Born into a farm family in the late 1940s, J.L. Fredrick lived his youth in rural Western Wisconsin, a modest but comfortable life not far from the Mississippi River. His father was a farmer, and his mother, an elementary school teacher. He attended a one-room country school for his first seven years of education.

Wisconsin has been home all his life, with exception of a few years in Minnesota and Florida. After college in La Crosse, Wisconsin and a stint with Uncle Sam during the Viet Nam era, the next few years were unsettled as he explored and experimented with life's options. He entered into the transportation industry in 1975 where he remained until retirement in 2012. He is a long-time member of the Wisconsin State Historical Society.

Since 2001 he has fourteen published novels to his credit, and two non-fiction history volumes, *Rivers, Roads, & Rails*, and *Ghostville*. He was a featured author during Grand Excursion 2004.

J.L. Fredrick is currently exploring the U.S. in an RV, and continues to write.

Made in the USA
Lexington, KY
31 July 2017